Chronicle of a Plague, Revisited

Chronicle of a Plague, Revisited

AIDS and Its Aftermath

Andrew Holleran

Da Capo Press

A Member of Perseus Books Group

New York

Designed by Pauline Brown
Set in 11.5 point Garamond by the Perseus Books Group

Library of Congress Cataloging-in-Publication Data
Holleran, Andrew.
  Chronicle of a plague, revisited : AIDS and its aftermath /Andrew Holleran.
    p. cm.
  "Some of the pieces in this collection originally appeared in *Ground Zero*, published in 1988 by William Morrow and Company, Inc."
  ISBN-13: 978-0-7867-2039-2 (alk. paper) 1. AIDS (Disease)—New York (State)—New York. 2. Male homosexuality—New York (State)—New York. I. Holleran, Andrew. Ground zero. II. Title.
  RA643.84.N7H65 2008
  614.5'993920097471—dc22

                                                                    2007053067

First Da Capo Press edition 2008

Published by Da Capo Press
A Member of the Perseus Books Group
www.dacapopress.com

Da Capo Press books are available at special discounts for bulk purchases in the United States by corporations, institutions, and other organizations. For more information, please contact the Special Markets Department at the Perseus Books Group, 2300 Chestnut Street, Suite 200, Philadelphia, PA 19103, or call (800) 810-4145, extension 5000, or e-mail special.markets@perseusbooks.com.

1 2 3 4 5 6 7 8 9

Contents

Introduction

LEARNING A BOOK is out of print is a blow to an author. It's not that the copies in print have been destroyed, but that demand for the book is so low the publisher cannot justify printing any more. When I went looking for a copy of *Ground Zero* last winter, I was lucky to find one in a college library in Washington, D.C., on a shelf of other books about AIDS. The "Date Due" slip told me the book had been checked out only twelve times in twenty-four years; and not at all from 1992 to 1998 or 1998 to 2006. This had to do with a professor teaching, then dropping, a course that required the text, I thought—what else keeps these books alive? The volumes on the shelf around mine looked equally untouched, as if they all had been put to sleep, like the awful time itself.

The awful time is what *Ground Zero* was about. I chose the title, long before 9/11, because it felt as if AIDS had exploded in New York like a bomb among gay men and left a crater in our lives. Now, however, Ground Zero means a real crater in Manhattan.

For this and other reasons, there seems to be little need to re-visit the years when AIDS arrived in New York. These essays are being reprinted, in fact, only because Dale Peck and the English editor Richard Canning were upset that certain books written during the AIDS epidemic by people like Allen Barnett, Harry Kondoleon, Christopher Coe, David Wojnarowicz, and John Weir not only were out of print but, they felt, had not received their due because of the times in which they were published. So they spoke to Don Weise, an editor at Carroll & Graf, about launching a series of reprints, a series now in abeyance because of the demise of that publisher. (*Ground Zero* was the only one that squeaked through.) What drew Weise to the project, however, is still valid: He was afraid that this part of gay history was being forgotten.

I realized I had forgotten life in New York in the eighties when I began looking through *Ground Zero*. In fact, what struck me immediately as I leafed through its pages in the college library was that New York in 1983 now seemed as exotic as ancient Egypt. It was like opening up a tomb to come upon quotes from people whose voices, scattered throughout the essays, I'd not heard in more than twenty years. I'd forgotten my roommate's telling me, "I don't like looking at pictures of dead people." I'd forgotten a friend saying, "I wasn't doing anything everyone else wasn't." Or another friend whispering to me at the baths, "The germs don't need me." But it was these voices of the dead that summoned up for me that awful time when no one could see the way out.

That no one could see the way out explains the essays in *Ground Zero*. In 1980 I was writing a column in the magazine *Christopher Street* called New York Notebook. *Christopher Street* was a new magazine founded by Charles Ortleb and Michael Denneny, among others, to provide a venue for writing about a subject (gay life) for which till recently it had been hard to find a home. Before AIDS hit, my column dealt with art exhibits, dance clubs, the music they played, and other minor issues of urban gay life. Then, around 1982, something called "the new gay cancer" appeared. I was not sure how to write about it. My first column on this topic ("Journal of the Plague Years") was a satire: a fantasy on cryogenics in which I imagined having oneself frozen till the unpleasantness was over and then awakened, like Rip Van Winkle or Walt Disney. Alas, this was not an option.

Instead, many people died; others took care of them; still others organized. Everybody was afraid. It's the latter emotion that pervades this book. A quarter of a century later, the essays in the original *Ground Zero* seem to me to be about three self-centered fears: Was I going to die? Would having sex kill me? And, What could I write about now? Laid end to end, these columns remind me of a reader who accused me of something the Jesuits call "morose delectation"—an addiction to melancholy. At the time I wondered if he was right; now this does not even seem a question.

In the end, I see now, I was one of those people who were frozen, if not cryogenically, by AIDS. I did not join Act Up; I did not write a play or memoir, or demonstrate; I moldered in a subset of gay men called "the worried well." Though the worried well did not think their worries worth attention (because they were not sick), as psychologist Clifford Odets pointed out later, such men had their own problems: survivors' guilt, withdrawal, and depression. Negative *and* negative, uninfected and pessimistic, I felt there was nothing we could do about AIDS except wait for a scientist to find a cure. Reading *Ground Zero* today, the monotony that permeates this collection of columns—published in a monthly magazine, but read here, back to back, in book form—seems exacerbated by a dreadful fatalism and a sense of impotence.

Writers feel impotent to begin with, I suppose—onlookers, not actors—but at no time did commentary seem more pointless than 1983. I had originally taken on the column in *Christopher Street* to solve a literary problem: the difference between nonfiction and fiction. I thought a nonfiction column might help me see what that was, and whether there was any point in writing fiction at all. By the time *Ground Zero* came out, in 1988, real life had trumped the question: Fiction seemed beside the point.

For what imagined story could match what was going on every day in gay New York in the eighties? The wish to pay someone to freeze you till it was over, like the mad scientist in one of Charles Ludlam's plays, made sense. Even Ludlam could not, I suspect, have imagined what finally happened to him. What happened to him, and was happening to others, was so bizarre that the first time I mentioned AIDS in my column I was afraid I would annoy readers (for the same reason hosts told guests not to bring it up at dinner). So I made sure to follow every column about AIDS with one that was light or funny. (Hence six satires on safe sex in the original book, which I've removed.) Eventually there was no need to apologize for mentioning AIDS—one had to apologize for not mentioning it—and, by 1986, I was writing only two kinds of essay: descriptions of New York–as–a–cemetery and elegies for friends.

When *Ground Zero* came out in 1988, a reviewer in San Francisco dismissed it as being too conventional. I agree. If the times demanded an extraordinary response, this wasn't one. Years later Andrew Sullivan would write a piece for the *Times* called "When Plagues End," which said that, now that there were anti-retrovirals, the plague was over, and AIDS was a manageable illness like diabetes. During the eighties there was no such comfort. Africans called AIDS "The Horror" for good reason. AIDS quickly converted people in their twenties into old men who were blind, mad, wasting away, racked with fevers, chills, pneumonia, diarrhea, Kaposi's sarcoma, dementia, and other diseases made possible by a total breakdown in the immune system. Living in New York, I wrote, felt like attending a dinner party at which some of the guests were being taken outside and shot, while the rest of us were expected to continue eating and making small talk. Let me update this: AIDS worked its way through gay New York with the malicious eye of the sectarians in Iraq—assassinating, it seemed, all the best people first. When the movie *Longtime Companion* came out, Vincent Canby denounced it in the *Times* for featuring only white, middle-class gay men, but they were in fact the group that AIDS first attacked in the United States.

To be more exact, the first targets of AIDS were Haitians, hemophiliacs, and homosexuals: not exactly the mainstream.

Perhaps that was why this new disease did not receive the immediate attention accorded, say, the pneumonia spread by a cooling system in a hotel in Philadelphia where a group of Legionnaires (white, middle-class, straight) had met. Perhaps that explains the ostracism and the panic—when TV crews refused to interview AIDS patients, and bodies were left unclaimed by funeral homes, and Pat Buchanan said gay teachers should be fired, and William Buckley Jr. suggested people with HIV have this status tattooed on their arms (something, ironically, the porn star/writer Scott O'Hara did years later, after he got tired of sex partners rejecting him when he told them he was Positive). African American churches refused to even discuss the subject, and only now, as I write, have the president of South Africa and his minister of health ended their policy of refusing to provide HIV medicine because—he claimed—AIDS is caused by poverty, not HIV, and—she said—it can be cured with a diet of beets and garlic. This nonsense, alas, is still going on as I write this, at the cost of numberless lives.

The schism between Africa and the West, however, was hardly worse than the division between gay Americans who had HIV (Positives) and those who did not (Negatives). This was not something I felt I could write about at the time, though early on it struck me that this difference trumped every other. That is why the writing in *Ground Zero* seems to me to have the frightened, solemn air of someone visiting an intensive care unit. When the dance critic Arlene Croce asked in *The New Yorker* how she was supposed to criticize a ballet about AIDS by a choreographer who had AIDS, she was predictably assailed for inquiring, but her question was valid. Who had the right to write about AIDS at all, much less make judgments? The only people, it seemed to me, with authority to do so were people with HIV.

In 1985 it was considered wrong, for instance, to discourage, much less stigmatize, people with AIDS, which led to practices that slighted not only basic tenets of public health (e.g., tracing of sexual contacts) but certain values on which literature depends, like candor. In other words, how could one impress on the Negatives the horror of AIDS without disheartening the Positives? The argument over what people with HIV should be called (*not* victims), the campaign to detach AIDS from homosexuality in the public mind, the drug companies' glossy ads that showed handsome young men with HIV perched on cliffs— as if having the virus were nothing more than a reason to go rock-climbing—were all a form of spin. Reality was much more disturbing. The argument that Gabriel Rotello made in his book *Sexual Ecology*—that until a core group of gay men stopped infecting others, the plague would go on—went unheeded, as did Larry Kramer's call to "Stop screwing!" There was, of course, a moral, if not scientific, solution to the epidemic from the start; yet it took decades before a slogan like "Let AIDS stop with me" could be used; and it is possible only now to say things that were considered unspeakable at the time.

AIDS silenced some writers, in fact, at the same time it freed others. Robert Ferro so resented the devouring of gay life by AIDS that he not only kept his own disease secret, but refused to even use the word in his last novel, for fear of letting this virus reduce his writing, too, to an aspect of the plague. Larry Kramer, on the other hand, not only helped found Act Up, but wrote *The Normal Heart*, *The Destiny of Me*, and *Reports from the Holocaust*. David Feinberg and John Weir burst on the scene with AIDS novels. Paul Monette, who'd been writing unproduced screenplays in Los Angeles, wrote a memoir (*Borrowed Time*); a book of poems (*Love Alone*); an autobiography (*Becoming a Man*) that won the National Book Award; and a final meditation, *Last Watch of the Night*, before dying. Others, like Randy Shilts, George Whitmore, David Wojnarowicz, Essex Hemphill, Samuel Delaney, and Alan Barnett, wrote nonfiction that many people consider their best work. Edmund White said the short story was the best fictional form in which to deal with AIDS and then proceeded to show why in "A Darker Proof." Felice Picano waited years before telling his story in his novel, *Onyx*. In the theater, William Hoffman, Harry Kondoleon, Scott McPherson, Craig Lucas, and Tony Kushner wrote plays that got considerable attention; even Charles Ludlam, we learn in his biography, considered *Salome*—a play in which he lay onstage in the robes and jewels of a Carthaginian princess, surrounded by a glistening pod of musclemen from the Sheridan Square gym—his response to the epidemic.

Ludlam in mascara, headdress, faux pearls, and breasts was a High Camp answer to a situation so horrible one did not know whether to make fun of it or be very, very serious. But in any case art was no substitute for a cure. There was something about AIDS that plays and books could not touch; the only thing, I wrote, people wanted to read was a single headline: CURE FOUND. Meanwhile lovers were jumping out of windows in suicide pacts or walking into moving traffic. Yes, the arts absorbed the new subject matter, but so what? At a writers' conference in Key West in 1993 called "Literature in the Age of AIDS," Tony Kushner began his remarks by saying he felt guilty being flown around the country to appear at arts festivals while people were dying. On the street, individual loneliness deepened despite the cultural response. Twenty-five years later I open a drawer in my bedroom to find a pair of socks and there, alongside my LITERATURE IN THE AGE OF AIDS T-shirt, is a heap of unused condoms sloshing around like a school of sardines; and I am transported back to a time when we regarded everyone as a potential killer.

The resulting personal isolation was an ironic counterpoint to the image of a gay community that AIDS coverage was painting for the American public at the time. Coverage of AIDS outed gay people and gay life—normalized them, at a terrible price: AIDS simultaneously destroyed that world as it was being revealed. The plague fragmented, Balkanized, gay people. Either you were sick or well; Positive or Negative; in Act Up or home reading; had friends who were sick or knew no one who was; could plan for the future or could not; had decided to stop having sex altogether or went on, with periodic bouts of worry. The fact that even nations could not agree on the risk of oral sex—Canada/Europe versus the United States—meant that everyone had to devise (and still devises) his own code of conduct. People were on their own. They scuttled about the battlefield as best they could, not knowing whom to trust: the voices that urged abstinence or the harangues of groups like Sex Panic, who argued that AIDS was nothing but a campaign to stamp out gay liberation; the forces that demanded the bathhouses be closed, or the voices that said they were the best venue for safe sex.

The final Balkanization of gay life, however, was that some of us lived, others died. "How wonderful it will be," a friend said to me one evening in the seventies, "when we get old—we'll all go from one house to the other, visiting!" I think he imagined everyone settled in little cottages up and down the Hudson. But friendships that would have evolved over time were tested by AIDS long before old age could. AIDS made people ask: What are we to one another? Even in New York, walking into a hospital and identifying oneself to the person at the desk, the word "friend" sounded flimsy. Then there was the final breach as you watched your friends burning up in a furnace you could not enter.

What a way to end one's life! Did it seem like life's final penalty for being homosexual? Few writers at the time spoke of the anger the sick felt toward those who were well, or the shame—a shame still evident in obituaries that refuse to list AIDS as the cause of death. There were lots of things not said during the worst years of the plague—but now that it has supplemented the gay white male community with the straight black and Hispanic population, not to mention whole continents, one wonders still if there is any overview that can be the final word. AIDS is now thought to belong to the Third World, to Asia and Africa, and, in this country, to the black and Hispanic communities. Twelve thousand people are infected every day worldwide; in the United States, one out of four infected does not know he or she carries it. Prevention has failed to stop the disease. In this country the issue no longer seems important. Yet last night, walking down Pennsylvania Avenue, a friend who's had HIV for over twenty years (and lost two partners to it) told me he'd started dating a man who got HIV in 2000 after having sex with someone who said he was Negative but wasn't. ("Don't ask, don't tell" describes more than a military policy the last few decades.)

It was strange having this talk in 2007 in Washington, D.C., after a relaxed Thanksgiving Day on which AIDS had seemed far away (except for the theater marquee we passed advertising a play by a man who'd died of It). But my friend's medications are starting to show signs of failure, and the new medications he wants are experimental, and before he can take them, they must find out what strain of the virus he has. A cell has two receptors, he explained as we walked past the White House; one strain of the virus attaches itself to one receptor, the other strain to the second, and one strain to both. The medicine he wants to take works only on the virus that attaches to one of the receptors. He has just taken a blood test that will require two months of processing to learn if that is the strain of HIV he has.

Listening to him I was struck, as I was so often in the past, by how much we know about the virus, leading to the question, So why can't we kill it? My friendships with the dead are idealized, I suppose, preserved in amber, no longer subject to the disagreements (or, conversely, the deepening intimacy) that would have occurred over the course of time had they lived. That's why those who do remain mean more than they might have otherwise. I feel a bond with this man simply because he has lived through all of this. There is a gratitude one has for people simply because they're still here.

There aren't that many when I go back now to the city of New York, which, after AIDS, after 9/11, has never seemed more prosperous, popular, and populous; though when I return it's another city, the city of 1983, the city in this book, that is the real one in my mind. I am past the point where seeing certain canopies and doorways reminds me of dead friends. New York is always dismantling itself anyway. That's why one friend's apartment is now part of the Whitney Museum annex, the Everard Baths is a Korean shopping center, the Club Baths a restaurant, and the building that housed The Saint—where I used to worry I might get HIV from brushing against the sweat of other dancers— part of NYU. The dome that used to float above the dance floor sits in a warehouse on Long Island, and the few friends still living in Manhattan are now dealing with the problems of aging. Act Up no longer demonstrates. Larry Kramer is writing a novel. Marathons, bike rides, walks to raise money for AIDS are not the command performances they once were. Young people still are seroconverting, but few seem outraged by the fact.

Yet it seems incredible that people still get infected with HIV. They say it's because people think AIDS is now a "manageable" disease; and few young gay men have seen anyone die of AIDS. But I think it's the same old story: the irrational power of sex, of people's search for a physical, emotional connection. So I suppose it should be no surprise that people go on getting infected, while books about AIDS sit mostly undisturbed on the shelf of the college library where I found *Ground Zero*. Even now I'm not sure what one should compare the disease that swept gay New York in the eighties to—the Spanish influenza of 1918? Maybe

AIDS will turn out to be regarded as only one of many viruses that will cull the enormous herd of mobile human beings that now populates our planet—like the incurable staph infection which, the *Times* reports today, caused more deaths in the United States in 2005 than AIDS, emphysema, Parkinson's, and traffic accidents combined. Perhaps the only reason AIDS caused such a stir in this country was that it intersected with a volatile subject: homosexuality.

Still, say what you will, we have lost a whole generation of gay men, who might otherwise have been valuable mentors to their successors. Of course, gay life has evolved without those who died. One can even argue that the very assimilation that AIDS brought about seems to have caused the disintegration of the gay community, though surely that would have resulted anyway from the inevitable change in generations, not to mention new technology like the computer. Part of Survivor's Syndrome is to live in another era, when AIDS is simply part of the past, and for many young gay men, not even that. Yet something was lost.

Last summer when a wildfire started in the Okefenokee Swamp, what's missing came back to me in a curious way. Away from Florida, I decided one morning when the fires were getting near my town that I should fly back immediately, put my papers in the car, and drive off so they would not burn up. Yet when it came time to decide which papers I would save, all I could think of was one of the essays I've added to this new edition—the record of a friend's battle with AIDS. Why? Because it seemed important that there be some record of what he went through. We are not entirely free of the dead. Years ago a friend who had been as skeptical as I about Act Up at the beginning, but started going to its meetings after deciding the protests had accelerated medical help, accused me—after his death, through a mutual friend—of not doing enough about AIDS. This has always bothered me. Last fall, reading the latest volume of Gore Vidal's memoirs, I came upon this line: "I am also chided for not doing enough about AIDS; but my virological skills are few." That's it. If a virus could only be stopped by a scientist, it seemed to me at the time, all the rest of us could do was stand by friends.

But even that was done in such various ways. Judgments about who did what during a crisis will always be with us; I have mine, too. But one comes back to the childhood fable about the symphony: Even the piccolo has its part. What I didn't realize at the time was something I learned watching people respond in individual ways: One contributes what one can. If the story of Act Up is the public history of AIDS, all these essays might do is supply a glimpse of the private side. The private side of AIDS was not exhilarating. I am proud of some of the writing in this new edition of *Ground Zero* but not of the sense of impotence. Morose delectation? Yes. And that sin the Catholics hold especially serious: despair—in other words, some of the things many of us were feeling when AIDS was inextricably bound up with fear. Here are a vanished time and place: gay New York, when no one knew the way out.

Circles

I MET COSMO his first year at the university in Philadelphia, my first in law school; our friendship was rooted in a time and place I considered idyllic even then. Life consisted simply of books and sports and long, clear twilights waiting for night to fall so one could go to the bars. I lived in a high-rise for graduate students a block from a brand-new gymnasium with an Olympic-sized pool and beautiful new squash courts. Cosmo lived a few blocks away in an apartment off campus, with a friend who was a dancer. The dancer was a bit snotty. Cosmo I liked from the start. He was a gymnast, and though gymnasts (and dancers) are, I often think, somewhat cold, he was not; he was reserved, poised, organized, but he was very good-hearted. He was small, but perfectly formed, in face and body; had Cosmo been tall, he would have been breathtaking. As it was, he was quite something. We both loved the gym. The gyms at that university were two: one small and brand new, the other cavernous and nineteenth-century. In the old gym, men swam naked in the marble pool, the locker room had a ceiling so high it was like a train station, and in the dim, gray air one would see athletes standing at the bottom of diagonal shafts of light as they removed their clothes, like the men at Thomas Eakins's *Swimming Hole*. The gymnasts had a huge room upstairs. Cosmo spent hours there, but I was afraid at first even to enter it. I had come to sports late in life, disliking them as a child, knowing, in my heart of hearts, as the baseball descended from the sky toward the ineffectual glove I held outstretched in my pessimistic hand, that I would not catch the ball, was not suited for baseball or the company of other boys. And years later I still had to overcome a great deal of fear and self-consciousness to enter a locker room and use the facilities of a gym, as if at any moment someone would recognize me as an imposter. But at a large university, in an enormous gym, self-consciousness dissipates. You are on your own. No team is going to groan when you miss the ball, and no parent is in the stands watching you play. You are left alone in a huge, sunny room, on a golden, polished floor, with a pair of chalk-whitened rings suspended in space, inviting you to try a muscle-up. That's where I met Cosmo.

Cosmo was the best at tumbling and mat exercises—back flips, handstands—but he was also expert enough on the stationary rings, and pommel horse, and parallel bars, to teach me those. My goal was a handstand on the rings and circles on the pommel horse. Cosmo was a patient teacher: cool, calm, humorous. Though he was far beyond my beginner's level in the sport he pursued with the thoroughness of a perfectionist, he was always willing to help. He seemed from the moment I met him master of things I wanted to learn. In fact, Cosmo awed me slightly, because, while six years younger than I, he seemed several years more poised. He was one of those people who strikes you, even in school, as knowing what they want. I did not. I would often leave the books on contracts and torts unread on my desk to go down to the gym in the middle of the afternoon and try hanging from the rings, balancing on the pommel horse, perfecting my handstand. Destiny—in that somnolent world of gyms and libraries—seemed more bound up with my body than my mind, though the guilt this engendered only increased an air of apology Cosmo was quick to make fun of. He had, besides a mania I did not share for puns, a somewhat wicked sense of humor.

Cosmo was not his real name. In high school, his classmates had nicknamed him Cosmopolitan; I think they must have been responding to that quality Cosmo had even before I met him: a certain self-possession. He came from a large midwestern city he expressed no particular desire to go back to. He seemed, on his ten-speed with his knapsack, utterly independent, as if all he needed in life were a combination lock, a Penguin paperback, and a can of V-8 juice. Even greater proof in my mind of his sterling character was his complete lack of interest in the bars downtown, which, like gyms, I had only recently discovered and could not get enough of. He did like to go to the beach, however, and the two of us went to Atlantic City together.

Atlantic City in 1970 was wonderfully seedy, in a physical, not moral, sense: crumbling, faded, forgotten; a ramshackle, salt-misted facade of huge hotels with grandiloquent European names (the Marlborough-Blenheim, the Chalfonte, Haddon

Hall), overlooking a brown beach and even browner surf. We were happy there—those long afternoons when the men hawking ice-cream sandwiches stomped about the hot sand in boots with thick soles and two pairs of cotton socks. Cosmo and I would lie on our blanket, talking in British accents, mine that of a BBC announcer, his that of a Cockney prostitute. Why I don't know. But all Cosmo had to do was blare some cheap sentiment in the voice of that British tart to crack me up—perhaps because Cosmo himself was so well-mannered an example of WASP reserve. In everything else (including the sensible manner in which he brought in his knapsack lotion, water, oranges, a Penguin paperback on Hinduism, extra money, clean T-shirt, hat), he was the soul of reason. So that when a momentary confusion about what to do with his life occurred that year, it did not surprise me when he resolved it quickly by deciding to study architecture. About the same time I left law school because I could no longer endure torts, Cosmo was accepted by Columbia, and when he moved to New York to study, I moved to New York to move to New York.

He praised the Columbia gym on the telephone; I joined a course in gymnastics at the West Side Y. From time to time I saw Cosmo downtown, including one morning on Avenue A when he introduced me to his new lover, a man who seemed to me a worthy catch—handsome, smart, with a sense of humor as dry, if not as wacky, as Cosmo's. He was also an architect, and when Cosmo graduated, he went downtown to work and live with him. The lover disliked sand. So Cosmo and I went to the beach together—first to Fire Island, and then to Jones Beach, because it seemed more convenient in the end. The lover was anxious and ambitious for the firm he had founded, and during those early lean years, I felt guilty calling on Cosmo. When I went to pick him up at the loft he shared with John, I felt slightly sub rosa, like a nine-year-old playmate who calls on a friend to take him out to do something naughty. Yet we were doing nothing so awful. All we did was what we'd done in Atlantic City: talk in British accents, laugh, and lie on our blanket discussing the bodies passing.

Cosmo admired the male body, and so did I. I was even more addicted to bars, beaches, and gyms than I'd been in Philadelphia. About the time I moved to the McBurney Y on Twenty-third Street, Cosmo joined the Sixty-third Street Y to work out with the gymnastics squad there. His body was always a shock to me when I saw it on the beach—without the wristbands, chalk whitening his hands, the worn gym shorts and T-shirt, the wire attached to a belt, which enabled him to learn a dismount from the rings without falling. His body—hardened to a fine edge through hours and hours of the painstaking repetition of certain moves that, unless they are done perfectly, do not count at all—was, like that of a ballet dancer, so tight, so chiseled, it seemed out of place against the blowsy, lazy, limitless stretch of soft sand, heaving sea. Yet Cosmo knew how to unwind: remove a banana from his knapsack, peel and eat it as if it were quite something else before turning to his suntan lotion. The contents of his knapsack never changed, nor did the contents of our friendship ("Would you do my back?"), which was why it meant so much to me: Cosmo was a link with the academic world I'd left behind in Philadelphia. He stood for all the things I still, at bottom, loved more than any others: books, wit, the body, a beach in summer, a friend to laugh with and sit beside on the train going back to the city—tired, spent, completely happy—as the big red sun winked between the buildings of Queens.

There was also something else about him, something morally solid, that I admired. One day when I mentioned my confusion about whether a blind person in public wants assistance or not, Cosmo said, "Just go up and ask them." He had an uncle who was blind. That Cosmo knew this etiquette did not surprise me, nor did the fact that his business finally prospered. I was proud when an apartment Cosmo and John had done was "published" in the *Times*. In fact, because Cosmo and John were witty, smart, good-looking, I always wanted to invite them to parties, introduce them to friends—but I never did. For one thing, they had no need of friends; they had each other. They wanted to meet clients, I suspected, and that was that. So I would, on my way home from the Y on Twenty-third Street (where I eventually moved), merely ring their buzzer and go upstairs to talk. We always had fun, and on one occasion Cosmo lent me a book he liked, *The Philosophy of Andy Warhol: From A to B and Back Again*.

It was not a book I particularly wanted to read—the one area in which I perhaps did have confidence was reading—but for some reason that evening I let him press it on me, thinking that if Cosmo found it special, I should check it out. It was another connection between us (just as friends who constantly borrow money from each other are, I sometimes think, only asking for proofs of affection). In fact it only confirmed my disinclination to borrow books. I read just a few pages and then put it beside my bed on the humidifier. People who borrow books, or money, or anything else, I've always felt, are under an obligation to return them as soon as possible; but I let Cosmo's loan gather dust beside my bed for quite some time because I thought I must be wrong about the book and intended to give it another chance. After all, Cosmo had recommended it.

In the meantime, as in some fairy tale, the years passed happily. I was published, Cosmo prospered, and we acquired what, when still in school, one fears one never will: a vocation and a source of income. We saw each other at the gym, or at the beach, riding back to town after those perfectly happy afternoons, with our knapsacks, sunburns, as the sun loomed very large and red beyond the dirt-encrusted windows and Cosmo—by merely widening his eyes over someone's conduct in the next row—broke me up. I forgot about the book; I forgot about the humidifier, an item which, when I bought it, had been touted as the magic means to moist skin and, months later, had been exposed as the means by which bacteria circulate through a room. We were very health conscious. So much for trends. Life proved as reversible as the function of the humidifier. The decade of—among other things—meeting Cosmo at Jones Beach, the baths, his loft, ended abruptly in 1983 when I was forced to leave Manhattan for family reasons.

For the next four years I did not see Cosmo; when I came back to the city on visits of one or two weeks, I walked by his loft overlooking Madison Square and looked up at the window and at the rings hanging from his ceiling. I thought often of pressing the buzzer and just dropping in. Just dropping in on friends as one walks around New York is one of its great plea- sures, but it's tricky, in a way: One doesn't want to drop in at the wrong time, or drop in and not be welcome. And the truth was I always called Cosmo; he never called me. So I'd sit for a while on a bench in Madison Square and look up at the window instead. During the years I was mostly out of New York, during the years his book lay beneath bags of manuscripts and plaster and dirty clothes, during the years I did not really know where I lived, and felt that I belonged neither to New York nor to the other places I stayed, I did not have the sort of ebullience one needs to drop in on people you don't see often. AIDS had arrived. People were dy- ing, people were changing, and stopping by to visit a friend meant talking not about the baths, the beach, the gym, but death. So I would merely think of ringing the bell; that's all; then leave town without doing it. Instead I sent Cosmo from Cleve- land one fall a clipping about a house there (because he grew up in Cleveland), and he sent me back a clipping about a project of his own in Manhattan, which struck that note of professional pride that made me feel I did not have that much in common with Cosmo anymore. For if youth lies on a beach discussing men with no thought of the morrow, middle age shrinks life to career.

Then one spring I returned to New York in a different mood. The changes that had been so painful seemed complete; people seemed to have constructed sane lives around the plague. When I did visit friends, we did not talk about It with the same leaden fi- nality at the end of every conversation. I even began to think that the worst was over and that those alive were the lucky survivors.

And one April afternoon, I cleaned my bedroom—the physical expression of a mental change—and came upon the book Cosmo had lent me nearly four years before.

It was clear to me now I wasn't going to read this book, and since I'd had it quite long enough, I decided that returning it was the perfect pretext to see Cosmo. But I did not rush to the phone. Why not? Because the four years that had passed since I'd seen Cosmo were not just any years; they were a sort of minefield. Then one day a friend got me into the McBurney Y, and not only did I recall, instantly, how for years in New York the gym was a source of pleasure, but I found myself growing mentally more confident about everything. And one afternoon I returned from a swim at the Y in so buoyant a mood my fears seemed simply silly. And I picked up the phone with only one worry: that I'd get the new scourge of New York—the answering machine.

Instead, I got a human voice, a gentle, smooth, resonant voice—typical of Cosmo and his crowd, in a way: calm, friendly, intelligent. I asked if Cosmo was there. "Cosmo?" he said. "Cosmo?" And I heard a shuffling of objects, a pause, as if he were looking around in embarrassment. Instantly, I thought, *Cosmo and John have split up. This is the new lover. The replacement.* Then he asked who was calling; I said I was an old friend. He said, "Cosmo died." Now, even the reception of bad news is accompanied by a thrill, a frisson—when a macabre premonition is fulfilled—and yet as I stood there trying to absorb this juxtaposition of subject and verb, discounting all the factors that pollute grief with vanity, and noting that I half suspected the news and was attracted, meanwhile, to the voice of the man on the phone who told me, even after reminding myself that everyone must die sometime, that there have been plagues in human history before, that our emotions really do not amount to much in the vast scheme of the universe, that billions of people have died before this and billions will after, there was still something about this two-word sentence. Each question I fired at the gentle voice on the phone was only an attempt to dilute the shock, by acquiring concrete details. I asked how, when, how long. For there seem to be two ways people die of AIDS: slow and fast. Cosmo was fast. Two weeks. No symptoms, pneumonia, boom. And part of what I was feeling was terror—since each time a friend dies of this thing, your own hunch that you will escape seems less and less rational. And part of this sadness was that I had no one to mourn with: None of my friends knew Cosmo; he was not part of my circle; he belonged to those sleepy days in Philadelphia that seemed so innocent now. I had no one to tell the news to and thus relieve the sting.

I asked how Cosmo's lover had taken it; the voice explained that he could never have spoken this way had John not been out of the office at that moment. But John was getting better. I said, "Do you still get calls like this, asking for Cosmo?" and he replied, "Not as often." I thanked him and hung up, and wandered into the next room with the words *Cosmo died* repeating in my mind, thinking Cosmo was not like everyone else. Cosmo was special. Sure, everyone is special in one sense; in another, everyone is not. I sat down at the table and stared at the *Times* I was reading before I made the call—the headlines describing the nuclear accident at Chernobyl; the radioactive cloud drifting across Europe; the story in section B that said that by the year 2000, New York City could be 60 percent Hispanic, black, and Asian American. In other words, the world, and the city, would go on evolving, developing, without Cosmo. And I sat there for some time until I decided, later that evening, to go back to the gym, as if in motion, exertion, the cool, athletic use of the body, I would let this shock dilute itself.

Downstairs the weather had changed; after a warm couple of April weeks—Cosmo had died in September—it was nippy again, like a fall night. The World Trade Towers twinkled in the blue dusk. The crowds surged down St. Marks Place. There was an enormous NYU dormitory going up on Third Avenue. The city was booming. Yet a small part, an individual cell, of Manhattan had been extinguished. Out of the huge honeycomb of the city I walked through, one chamber was empty. Okay. By now we are so accustomed to obituaries, they have become a literary genre—and the fact is, the thirtieth death of a friend does not shock you as much as the first did. While much may be behind us (the initial shock, confusion, blame, numbness), one thing is not—everything may be over but the dying. That will go on. Even so, Cosmo's death horrified me. What a waste! What an insult! Having heard so many theories by which people explain what is still the inexplicable (why some die, others do not), I could only think they were utterly inapplicable to this one. I didn't think his death fit any theory, or moral judgment, or pop-psychological hypothesis (that those who die hate themselves, or are emotionally blocked, or unable to love, or ashamed of being homosexual—or any of the other current placebos circulating with increasing seriousness). It's not surprising, as science putters away in laboratories we have no access to, dropping, on the community far below, articles in journals and newspapers, that the two worlds—one of the lab, the other of the frightened heart—separate further from one another. But Cosmo loved life, treasured his body, was only thirty-five, succeeded in his career, and had much to look forward to. He didn't hate himself, sex, or life. His death did not illumine anything that leaves us morally edified, or superior, or enlightened—it was just part of the vast human waste that is occurring; just mean and nasty.

And though I knew that eventually I would recover from the shock of calling him to return his book and learning that he was dead, and though I knew this evening I would enjoy my visit to the gym, my optimism—my feeling it was over—was gone. I walked through Union Square up Broadway with a grim expression compressing my lips. All the half-baked theories that ostensibly applied to Cosmo swirled in my mind. None of them worked. I felt more and more despair. And then (as if to supply a literary symmetry to the day), when I got on the track at the Y, I glanced down and saw the gymnastics group working out on the floor beneath—including one handsome Hispanic man doing circles on the pommel horse. Circles are hard to do: You grasp the handles on the pommel, lift yourself up, and swing your legs around above the handles. When it is done well, it looks effortless; the legs themselves seem to be propelling themselves around, faster and faster, as the gymnast moves his hands and travels up and down the horse. It is fluid, graceful, exhilarating. I never learned to do more than one or two, which is to say I never learned circles—though Cosmo did. When I came to New York this spring, I felt we were moving forward—the worst behind us—but now, as the words *Cosmo died* play over and over again in my mind, I think, running ovals around the man doing circles on the pommel horse beneath, in the gym Cosmo loved, *we are getting nowhere at all; we are going in circles.* A pun Cosmo would have liked.

Bedside Manners

"THERE IS NO difference between men so profound," wrote Scott Fitzgerald, "as that between the sick and the well." There are many thoughts that fill someone's head as he walks across town on a warm July afternoon to visit a friend confined to a hospital room—and that is one of them. Another occurs to you as you wait for the light to change and watch the handsome young basketball players playing on the public court behind a chicken-wire fence: Health is everywhere. The world has a surreal quality to it when you are on your way to the hospital to visit someone you care for who is seriously ill. Everyone in it, walking down the sidewalk, driving by in cars, rushing about on a basketball court with sweat-stained chests, exhausted faces, and wide eyes, seems to you extremely peculiar. They are peculiar because they are free, walking under their own power, nicely dressed, sometimes beautiful. Beauty does not lose its allure under the spell of grief. The hospital visitor still notices the smooth chests

29

of the athletes in their cotton shorts as they leap to recover the basketball after it bounces off the rim. But everything seems strangely quiet—speechless—as if you were watching a movie on television with the sound turned off, as if everyone else in the world but you is totally unaware of something: that the act of walking across York Avenue under one's own power is essentially miraculous.

Every time he enters a hospital, the visitor enters with two simultaneous thoughts: He hates hospitals, and only people working in them lead serious lives. Everything else is selfish. Entering a hospital he always thinks, *I should work for a year as a nurse, an aide, a volunteer helping people, coming to terms with disease and death.* This feeling will pass the moment he leaves the hospital. In reality the visitor hopes his fear and depression are not evident on his face as he walks down the gleaming, silent hall from the elevator to his friend's room. He is trying hard to stay calm.

The door of the room that the receptionist downstairs has told the visitor his friend is in is closed—and on it are taped four signs that are not on any of the other doors and are headlined, WARNING. The visitor stops as much to read them as to allow his heartbeat to subside before going in. He knows—from the accounts of friends who have already visited—he must don a robe, gloves, mask, and even a plastic cap. He is not sure if the door is closed because his friend is asleep inside or because the door to this room is always kept closed. So he pushes it open a crack and peers in. His friend is turned on his side, a white mound of bed linen, apparently sleeping.

The visitor is immensely relieved. He goes down the hall and asks a nurse if he may leave the *Life* magazine he brought for his friend and writes a note to him saying he was here. Then he leaves the hospital and walks west through the summer twilight as if swimming through an enchanted lagoon. The next day— once more crossing town—he is in that surreal mood, under a blue sky decorated with a few photogenic, puffy white clouds, certain that no one else knows . . . knows he or she is absurdly, preposterously, incalculably fortunate to be walking on the street. He feels once again that either the sound has been turned off or some other element (his ego, perhaps with all its anger, ambition, jealousy) has been removed from the world. The basketball players are different youths today but just as much worth pausing to look at. He enters the hospital one block east more calmly this time and requests to see his friend—who is allowed only two visitors at a time, and visits lasting no more than ten minutes. He goes upstairs, peeks around the door, and sees his friend utterly awake. The visitor's heart races as he steps back and puts on the gloves, mask, cap, and robe he has been told his friends all look so comical in. He smiles because he hopes the photograph that made him bring the copy of *Life* to the hospital—Russian women leaning against a wall in Leningrad in bikinis and winter coats, taking the sun on a February day—has amused his friend as much as it tickled him.

"Eddie?" the visitor says as he opens the door and peeks in. His friend blinks at him. Two plastic tubes are fixed in his nostrils, bringing him oxygen. His face is emaciated and gaunt, his hair longer, softer in appearance, wisps rising above his head. But the one feature the visitor cannot get over are his friend's eyes. His eyes are black, huge, and furious. Perhaps because his face is gaunt or perhaps because they really are larger than usual, they seem the only thing alive in his face; as if his whole being were distilled and concentrated, poured, drained, into his eyes. They are shining, alarmed, and—there is no other word—furious. He looks altogether like an angry baby—or an angry old man—or an angry bald eagle.

And just as the hospital visitor is absorbing the shock of these livid eyes, the sick man says in a furious whisper, "Why did you bring me that dreadful magazine? I hate *Life* magazine! With that stupid picture! I wasn't amused! I wasn't amused at all! You should never have brought that dreck into this room!"

The visitor is momentarily speechless: It is the first time in their friendship of ten years that anything abusive or insulting has ever been said; it is as astonishing as the gaunt face in which two huge black eyes burn and shine. But he sits down and recovers his breath and apologizes. The visitor thinks, *He's angry because I haven't visited him till now. He's angry that he's here at all, that he's sick.* And they begin to talk. They talk of the hospital food (which he hates), of the impending visit of his mother (whose arrival he dreads), of the drug he is taking (which is experimental), and of the other visitors he has had. The patient asks the visitor to pick up a towel at the base of the bed and give it to him. The visitor complies. The patient places it across his forehead—and the visitor, who, like most people, is unsure what to say in this situation, stifles the question he wants to ask, *Why do you have a towel on your forehead?* The patient finally says, "Don't you think I look like Mother Teresa?" And the visitor realizes his friend has made a joke—as he did years ago in their house on Fire Island, doing drag with bedspreads, pillowcases, towels, whatever was at hand. The visitor does not smile—he is so unprepared for a joke in these circumstances—but he realizes, with relief, he is forgiven. He realizes what people who visit the sick often learn: It is the patient who puts the visitor at ease. In a few moments his ten minutes are up. He rises and says, "I don't want to tire you." He goes to the door and once beyond it he turns and looks back. His friend says to him, "I'm proud of you for coming."

"Oh—!" the visitor says and shakes his head. "Proud of *me* for coming!" he tells a friend later that evening, after he has stripped off his gown and mask and gone home, through the unreal city of people in perfect health. "Proud of me! Can you imagine! To say that to me, to make *me* feel good! When he's the one in bed!" The truth is he is proud of himself the next time he visits his friend, for he is one of those people who looks away when a nurse takes a blood test and finds respirators frightening. He is like almost everyone—everyone except these extraordinary people who work in hospitals, he thinks, as he walks into the building. The second visit is easier, partly because it is the second, and partly because the patient is better—the drug has worked.

But he cannot forget the sight of those dark, angry eyes and the plastic tubes and emaciated visage—and as he goes home that evening, he knows there is a place whose existence he was not aware of before: the foyer of death. It is a place many of us will see at least once in our lives. Because modern medicine fights for patients who a century ago would have died without its intervention, it has created an odd place between life and death. One no longer steps into Charon's boat to be ferried across the River Styx—ill people are now detained, with one foot in the boat and the other still on shore. It is a place where mercy looks exactly like cruelty to the average visitor. It is a place that one leaves, if one is only a visitor, with the conviction that ordinary life is utterly miraculous, so that, going home from the hospital on the subway, one is filled with things one cannot express to the crowd that walks up out of the station or throngs the street of the block where he lives. But if the people caught in the revolving door between health and death could speak, would they not say—as Patrick Cowley reportedly did as he watched the men dancing to his music while he was fatally ill, "Look at those stupid queens. Don't they *know?*" Guard your health. It is all you have. It is the thin line that stands between you and hell. It is your miraculous possession. Do not throw it away for the momentous pleasures of lust, or even the obliteration of loneliness.

Many homosexuals wonder how they will die: where, with whom. Auden went back to Oxford, Santayana to the Blue Nuns in Rome. We are not all so lucky. Some men afflicted with AIDS returned to die in their family's home. Others have died with friends. Some have died bitterly and repudiated the homosexual friends who came to see them; others have counted on these people. Volunteers from the Gay Men's Health Crisis have cooked, cleaned, shopped, visited, taken care of people they did not even know until they decided to help. We are discovering the strength and goodness of people we knew only in discotheques or as faces on Fire Island. We are once again learning the awful truth Robert Penn Warren wrote years ago: "Only through the suffering of the innocent is the brotherhood of man confirmed." The most profound difference between men may well be that between the sick and the well, but compassionate people try to reach across the chasm and bridge it. The hospital visitor who conquers his own fear of something facing us all takes the first step on a journey that others less fearful than he have already traveled much further on. As for the courage and dignity and sense of humor of those who are sick, these are beyond praise, and one hesitates where words are so flimsy. As for a disease whose latency period is measured in years, not months, there is no telling which side of the line dividing the sick and the well each of us will be on before this affliction is conquered. We may disdain the hysteria of policemen and firemen who call for masks, and people who ask if it is safe to ride the subway, and television crews who will not interview AIDS patients. For they are not at risk—those who are, are fearlessly helping their own.

Snobs at Sea

SOMEWHERE IN *Remembrance of Things Past*—which is to say, for the reader unable to find the line, somewhere in Russia, or the Amazon—the shock of learning that a rich man has fallen in love with a prostitute is compared to the trouble we have believing a man can die of a common bacillus. It's a double metaphor—comparing the course of love with the course of disease (Proust's favorite link), and social snobbery with the biological superiority human beings feel to other forms of life. The idea that an intelligent man with aristocratic friends, a fortune, family, career, can fall for a kept woman—or, in our day, be converted to a jar of ashes on the bookshelf by the action of an organism invisible to the naked eye—is somehow very hard for us to grasp. "The germs don't need me," said a friend at the baths one evening when I asked him if he wasn't worried about dying. "If they needed me, I'd be worried, but they don't need me."

In his metaphor the germs are hostesses making up guest lists for dinner parties, I guess—yet "The germs don't need me" is perhaps only the craziest version of a denial that a lot of us have practiced over the last two years, even while the people we have played with over the last decade and a half keep disappearing. We haven't, really, somehow, believed in this germ. However, the last line of a letter tells me as an afterthought that the weather of March 29 in New York was snow and sleet, "Perfect for Ray's funeral." I did not know Ray was sick, much less dead. This evening I am told on the telephone that Michael won't live past the weekend; CMV virus is running riot through his system, he is bleeding internally. But Michael went to *Cornell*, I think when I put down the phone; came from a good family; has a little garden on East Seventh Street he was always asking me to come see; was someone I have always had a crush on. What did the germs need with him?

He was, after all, a talented architect who had come to New York after college to work and enjoy himself—a modest agenda in the scheme of things. We met because I liked his roommate—a scientist with Bell Labs who took a class in gymnastics I attended at the West Side Y. Our first outing ended with my being dropped off in a taxicab at my corner, while Michael, in the backseat, smiled a knowing grin as I bid his roommate good night—as if Michael knew exactly what had, or had not happened; as if he were saying, "This one isn't what you think he is." Or, "You got no further than any of the others who've tried." His roommate eventually grew tired of the commute from Manhattan to southern New Jersey and vanished from the city. Michael stayed.

What struck me about Michael—the first time we went home together—was that, in contrast to his roommate, he was easy. Very easy. So easy that the fact that our attempts at sex failed in no way affected the affection we felt for each other. Michael was good-natured. Had a good sense of humor. And was less sexually inhibited than most people.

This was not, in the seventies, something that lowered him in my estimation—nor any of the other friends I had who went out searching for whatever we were searching for with a determination approaching dementia. Sex was partly what we had come to New York for, from families, universities, small towns, other cities. I'd come upon Michael summer nights with his lover, floating down a near-empty Broadway on bicycles; they spoke of moving to a farm in upstate New York, or Georgia, but never seemed to manage to. I would see him instead on the beach at Fire Island. Or on the sidewalk in front of my apartment, buying flowers, on his way home from work. Or in a room at the St. Mark's Baths. The last time I'd seen him at the baths, in fact, I'd walked into his room before I realized the body was his; and then, in a split second of recognition, two steps from his pillow, we both laughed. It was a compliment, in a way—freed of the formalities of friendship, stripped of his social identity and clothes, Michael was so desirable I'd taken the risk of stepping through the door. That door, of course, had been open to anyone who passed; there was something concupiscent, lascivious about Michael. The sheets he lay on were rumpled and damp with use, the lightbulb by the doorway red, the skin of his body shining with a film of oil. This greasy red chamber of love that eventually ended up as part of the towering heap of garbage on the sidewalk outside the St. Mark's Baths was something he made jokes about when I met him in a suit and tie there the next day, coming home from work: black plastic bags filled with the detritus of lovemaking, cans of Crisco, lubricant, poppers, paper plates, cups, packs of cigarettes—the whole effluvia of a disposable culture that had decided to dispose of sex the same way the Japanese restaurant a few doors down got rid of its grease.

Time magazine called it a sexual revolution (which it then declared *finito* in March 1984). Whatever it was—the pent-up frustration of lonely years in high school; the delayed release of urges that had been a source of anxiety and fear since puberty; or just the mating instinct in a new context—Michael exemplified its inexhaustible energy. He had first fallen in love with a professor at Cornell—a married man who left his wife for him and then went back to her—and I imagined Michael searching ever since in the baths for some recapitulation of this youthful love affair. No doubt that was romantic. But in a way the whole phenomenon was. I pictured a line of Yeats's chiseled above the doorway of the public clinic on Ninth Avenue where Michael and I went to have our stools analyzed, our blood tested. "Love has pitched its mansion in the place of excrement." Curious location. But then whatever one came down with could be cured. If we were playing on a garbage dump—that heap of black plastic bags on the sidewalk Monday mornings on St. Marks Place—it was under control. Penicillin had made sex possible, the way plastic paved the way for swimming pool liners and airplane seats. It made accessible to the average man a dream of sexual paradise previously confined to the canvases of Delacroix, the pages of *The Arabian Nights*. When we saw the red tea tent of an Indian mogul at the Metropolitan Museum in the India exhibit, it reminded Michael of the billowing pavilions people set up on Fire Island: a silken dream of Eros.

It was just that connection between art and life, history and the present, civilization and Eros, that Michael appreciated—his favorite things were art and sex. Paintings, sculpture, architecture—and bodies. One hot afternoon when the beach on Fire Island was closed to swimmers because the sewage that our Baghdad dumped off the coast had drifted dangerously close to land, Michael and I talked for a while beside the sweltering sea. All around us the crowd of men broiled in the sun, beside an ocean they could not enter. Unreal sea! It looked in fact perfectly beautiful, immense, invigorating—so green I stood skeptically at the edges for almost an hour before I saw the first tiny fleck of raw sewage, like a jellyfish in a transparent wave, floating in to shore. Only then did I give up thoughts of swimming and go back. There was no way to know this day—all of us marching up and down beside the polluted sea—was the future. "There's nothing worse than an ocean you can't swim in," Michael said as we returned to town on the nearly empty train. "Unless it's people you can't sleep with," he added with a smile. "I guess that's why the baths are so . . . relaxing."

Years before, a man had told me in a restaurant on Fifty-seventh Street that a doctor he knew was predicting a tremendous epidemic of typhus in the gay community—but it seemed at the time, over chicken salad sandwiches, just an instance of an ancient paranoia, a biblical vision of punishment-for-sex. No one *I* knew had typhus. Nor did I know that eventually not the outer but the inner ocean would turn foul: the sea of fluids that composed us. Little did we dream, nights at the Saint, when sweat was licked off dancers' bodies and kisses were exchanged, that years later we would refuse to drink from the water fountain there because of a new gay cancer. It took a while for people to believe in the invisible—the germ—for the same reason it took the nineteenth century a while to accept Pasteur's explanation of smallpox; but once accepted, the implications were mind-boggling.

It was thought when this began that those exposed to the virus—"infected" was somehow too harsh a word at the time—were simply the very reckless; the extraordinarily debauched. Then, as the numbers mounted, it seemed they were not very different from you and me. And the next popular hypothesis arose: Everyone had met these germs, but only some would succumb. (People were not ready to believe you could catch cancer the way you caught hepatitis.) When Michael got sick, he would stop and talk outside the baths on my block on his way home from work, and save for the fact that he no longer went in himself, he seemed perfectly normal. His illness did not upset me because its effects were not visible. He even seemed to be recovering under the care of a nutritionist. The only change I could see was that he seemed to wear a coat and tie more often—and he discussed his T-cell count, the results of his latest blood test. He was the example I reserved in my mind to prove it could be beaten, or at least lived with; it was not this fatal, fantastic, unbelievable thing it seemed to be. Eddie was going up to Sloan-Kettering every other day for the most avant-garde and technological of treatments, ever ready to try the new and the sophisticated. Michael, on the other hand, credited a macrobiotic diet with bringing his T-cell count back to normal (for a homosexual, that is; there were three categories, he told me with an ironic smile: Virgin, Average Man, and Homosexual). We laughed at this odd reminder that being the third, we were not the first two. He had his setbacks. One evening on his way to one of those Christmas parties New Yorkers give that, we agreed, are sometimes pointless and fatiguing, he was tired before even getting there; he'd just recovered from a bad day and was still angry that his lover had not brought him the soup he'd asked for, when he could not get out of bed. His life was quieter now, but by no means over; in fact, his work—his career as an architect—had prospered. He no longer went to the baths or Fire Island. He went to Rome instead that spring and, on his return, began to paint the ceiling of his apartment with a fresco found in a church or palace there—an admirable whimsy, it seemed to me, like Michael himself, like art these days—half-jest, half-glory. He seemed, in short, to have changed his habits—which consisted now of work, macrobiotic diet, and sitting in the garden he kept inviting me over to see, the garden I wanted to, meant to, see but did not because it was just a few blocks away and I would surely see it some evening.

Instead we sat on the stoop across from the baths on my block—which continued to draw men from all over the city and country—and watched people go in and out. "They want to commit suicide," said Michael. "In a few months they'll all be sitting in a doctor's office." The people at the baths said, "All life is risk." Homosexual men were either Puritan or Cavalier, and it all depended on your attitude toward something we could not see.

Before Michael died, I sometimes went into the baths and sat at the counter of the little restaurant to see the men going by the doorway in their towels—the baths, after all, were supremely visual—and sometimes, having seen a certain man go by the doorway in his towel, checked in myself and hung around the hallways in the darkness for a couple of hours, watching people I had not seen in some time, people who reminded me of the men you ran into at the Everard in 1971—and not only reminded me—since some of them were those men.

They were as improbable and beautiful lying in their rooms in their Jockey shorts and towels as the gods Michael had painted on his ceiling on Seventh Street—a burst of beauty, fantasy, art— in the midst of a nightmare reality. The thrill of homosexuality is finally an aesthetic thrill. They lay there exactly as I wanted them to; not so much gods floating on celestial clouds as river deities, lying on the shore of some sacred stream between the mud and the bulrushes. Dark, gritty, salubrious mud. "Life is risk," one said. "I don't care if I die tomorrow." Or, "The germs don't need me." And, "You can't stop living." But of course you can. It still seems against nature, a violation of the hierarchy of things, that a microbe could destroy a man who could stop on a summer evening and talk about friends, Rome, Christmas, while the city he loved went past us. It still seems a scandal that an item scientists do not even define as living—a microbe that can't paint angels, trumpets, clouds, or gods upon a ceiling—can devour a creature who can. It still seems a reproach that a virus can return us from the twentieth century to the Stone Age. Yet that is the revolution this thing has effected; that is the toppling that has occurred—the world turned upside down. Human beings lie broken and shattered on the ground, like statues pulled down by barbarians invading Rome, or Protestants smashing the art in a cathedral. The basilica's empty. The church is closed. Michael— who went to Cornell—is gone. And sometime this summer, some ignorant tenant will move into that apartment, unpack his bags, kill the first cockroach, lie down to rest, and find himself staring in surprise at a host of gods and goddesses, angels bearing trumpets, golden clouds—all painted by a man the germs needed, for what I do not know.

The Room

THE ROOM HAS a view of the East River; it's on the fourteenth floor. I sit there beside a thick plate glass window in silence and watch the barges and tugboats go by in both directions. Rising up from the flatness of Long Island City, across the river from Manhattan, is the steel skeleton of a mammoth skyscraper being built by Citibank, probably to hold canceled checks—a forecast of what will eventually be another Manhattan over there, since Manhattan seems to have doubled itself each time I come back. On the very edge of the island below, landing and taking off from a ledge concealed by the expressway built out over the river— FDR Drive—are helicopters. Two kinds: large white ones with red stripes that resemble the markings of the Coast Guard; and small black ones that take off in twos and threes and bring to mind a movie with James Bond. They're so American, somehow: our nervous energy, our impatience and desire to dip in and flee, our technology, our short attention span. I sit there and watch them take off and cross each other's flight paths, avoiding what looks like inevitable collision, and the sight is mesmerizing. The room is so quiet, the view so glorious, the sight of the soundless river traffic something one could sit watching for hours—mainly because the patient in the bedroom is at the moment fast asleep.

I think he is asleep; he may be waking, or just lying there, too tired to speak—whichever, he is covered in blankets, but still shivering as the onset of another fever takes hold. It's odd to see him shivering. We are in the center of the medical universe. This hospital is the state of the art. It's more like a luxurious hotel, in fact: a living room, a bathroom, and a bedroom with twin beds, so the patient and a family member or a friend can stay here with him. Upstairs and downstairs, on the other floors, are the doctors and machinery that represent the farthest medical science has gone in our century. The patient has just had a CAT scan and a spinal tap, and blood tests are being run to find out if some bacteria other than tuberculosis is causing these persistent fevers.

Outside the helicopters come and go with a frequency that suggests that time is never wasted in this city, or at least not in this neighborhood. Anything may happen in the next five minutes. Last night, a friend in Berlin told me that in Germany they think the answer to AIDS will come from the United States. I tell him that my friends and I, a few years ago, thought the answer would come from France. We imagined some eccentric Gallic genius, some Madame Curie, would see the tiny clue our bureaucratic institutes could not and shout *"Voilà!"* Odd, that no one says a word today about HPA-23, the drug that sent Rock Hudson over to Paris in his last days. No one says much about any of the drugs that we thought would be the treatment that worked—including AZT, which the *New York Native* now says killed Robert Joffrey. Who knows?

On the table here is the *AIDS Newsletter*, a publication that discusses treatments and drugs for the opportunistic illnesses that come in new batches every year. In Key West, a friend tells me, the leading doctor plays tapes of Louise Hay and everyone sits around like children in kindergarten singing, "I love myself." But most of us wait wherever we are for science to give us the answer, even when the thoughts and emotions raised by the spectacle of suffering seem (though one does not want to admit it in this secular age) religious.

But what religion? On the table by the window where I sit watching helicopters land and take off is a paperback copy of *Kalki* by Gore Vidal. *Kalki* is, I think, about the end of the world—the last line is "I am Siva." It feels, sitting here, as if this is the end of everything: a culture with infinitely subtle and complex technology made useless by something so primitive it is a question whether or not a virus constitutes Life. It certainly seems to make Life do whatever it wants. Inside the bedroom it is inducing in my friend Michael temperatures that have nothing to do with the warm spring day outside. He huddles on this April afternoon—when all the trees in Central Park are in new leaf, and the streets of the Village are jammed with handsome men in muscles and T-shirts, and people are sunbathing on the piers—while his body shakes under five bedspreads as the virus, or the bacteria it has allowed to proliferate, instills a deep chill into his bones. He might as well be in an igloo. He's shivering, shuddering, shaking, and it won't stop. Tomorrow more tests, and results of tests. He fights each battle as it comes. While outside the helicopters come and go in the shining sunlight, and the barges push their container cargo up and down the river, we sit perched in an aerie of what is perhaps the richest and most sophisticated city in the world in the bedroom of a man shivering like some victim of malaria in a little village in Panama in 1910.

I feel, watching these helicopters land and take off in perfect silence beyond the thick plate glass, the way I feel most of the time now in New York: not there. So much that is horrible has happened, one goes numb inside—one sits there, like the doctors, with no answers. We keep waiting for the tide to turn; statistics say the current growth in cases will be among drug addicts in the inner cities; but why then do more people I know have it each time I return to New York? This division that the test has set up—between Positives and Negatives—seems increasingly like so much nonsense. The news about AIDS, it seems, has always held two contradictory strains: (1) It's difficult to get (Then why do so many have it? And why are they predicting such huge numbers by 1991?); and (2) they know more about the AIDS virus than any other in history (Then why can't they stop it?).

Depending on which person you talk to, the theory on the street is: (1) Only bottoms get this; or (2) every one of us has been infected (the word used to be "exposed") by something that, given the variety and number of the sick, we must have picked up off the banister or doorknob, and before this decade is very old, every one of us is going to be in this room, or some much crummier version of it. (Hence anxiety attacks.) The fact is that whatever happens, those who are in this room now, or out (on leave, you might say), are fighting battles whose lessons will teach those who follow. They are the veterans Emmanuel Dreuilhe speaks of in his book, *Mortal Embrace*. His metaphor is that of war, and he is exactly right.

There is another book called *Borrowed Time* by Paul Monette, which is also about the skirmishes in this room, this room that is replicated more or less in so many towns and cities in this country, which, when you finish it, makes you think: No one who reads this can be the same afterward. Finally, we have a portrait of the hysteria, nobility, and suffering. Both books are very important. They're both about the attempt to repel each assault as it comes, which is what the shivering patient in the bedroom is engaged in. "I just want him a little while longer," whispered Robert, Michael's partner, before he left the room to do some errands, and I think: This is only the first, the first of many battles.

Yet it's strangely peaceful here; far more peaceful, in a way, than any other place in the city. The plague is not some dreaded amalgam of guilt and superstition that deforms our lives with anxiety and worry, some hidden assassin; it's here, out in the open, in this room. Michael asks me, when I go in, to turn his pillow—that pillow that grows overheated and stale when you are lying on it with a fever for a long time—but then I'm released back into the living room, whose flowers and books and magazines I ignore to watch the helicopters instead. Easy duty. When Robert returns from his errands, we try to talk about the funny things that have happened to us both since we last saw each other, but we talk a bit too fast, and finally I'm relieved when Michael asks us to be quiet because the talk is tiring him. The awkwardness we feel then soon evaporates; the reality is faced; the blessed silence of the place returns.

"Had your fill yet of New York?" Robert asks next in a very soft voice.

"No," I say. "I'd love to stay a few months."

"Really?" he said. "I'd get out in a minute if I could. When Michael gets over this, I want to go."

"Where?" I ask.

"Someplace dry," he says, "and hot." (The longing of people with tuberculosis; the dream of D. H. Lawrence.) "I've just got to get away. And we will. But I don't know where." Then he looks over at me and says, in an even softer voice, "It's so bad"—just once; his only reference to the fact of his heroic efforts to help his partner.

Finally Robert leaves to return to their apartment—the only time in two weeks he has left—and I sit here in the deep plush silence while he's gone, staring at the river, watching cars, boats, and helicopters move back and forth across the landscape.

The radio in the bedroom is playing very softly—some concert by the New York Philharmonic, a symphony by Scriabin. The angst of modern music, the despair of artists, seems silly in a room like this. "The cure for metaphysical pain," writes a friend of Paul Monette's in *Borrowed Time*, "is physical pain." So much for Scriabin. I could not listen to this music in the best of circumstances, but Michael wants the radio left on, like the lamp or fire an invalid needs to provide a sign of life, of warmth, in his sickroom. He cannot watch, on the other hand, television. He is infuriated by the evening news, the daily fare of New York City: the black teenager upstate whose story of being raped by white policemen seems with each passing day to have been made up; the hijacking of a Kuwaiti airliner; the gridlock in Palestine; the daily beatings, murders, scams the local news feeds us for our delectation because, whatever else crime and disaster are, they are dramatic. Too dramatic for a man fighting for a moment's rest from the onslaught the bacteria are waging.

"I'll be brave, I'll be brave," he says through chattering teeth. Then the little beep that says it's time to take his AZT goes off; he puts a hand out of the blanket to get two pills and swallows them. Imagine life broken into segments of four hours. Trapped in this technological nightmare, he goes forward with whatever weapons are handed him. And I sit down again to watch the helicopters.

Not that many people visit this room—partly because the patient has chosen not to tell most of his friends he is ill. Only now, when help is needed, does he think about widening the circle of those who know. Another friend who came here earlier today lost his own lover recently; he made wisecracks and gave the patient a massage with an irreverence, a black humor, that made me think: The more you live through this, the less august it seems. But he does not come back again; I suspect he's had enough of it for one lifetime. The details of these battles differ, but it is the same war. The instinct is to just stay home. A friend dressing for yet another wake recently stopped, took off his coat, and said, "I'm not going to another single one of these, ever." The photographer who's spent the past three years photographing people with AIDS is now taking pictures of rich people's llamas.

Even the people in this room long for their moments of escape—the sweetest passages in *Borrowed Time* are the lulls between the crises. Watching the helicopters is like that. Surely with all this energy, and wealth, and technology, you think as they fly off, we can find the solution to this thing. Surely the city that can build these buildings, highways, ledges for helicopters to dart on and off of, can defeat whatever is making the patient in the next room shiver and burn at the same time. Yet the city this room perches above is such a mix. The beggars who are everywhere, the Senegalese who unpack their bottles of perfumes and incense on tables in the subway, the panhandlers and youths who spend all night on St. Marks Place standing above a blanket covered with old porn magazines and books, remind us of a Third World from which this city can hardly hold itself aloof. "We Are the World" seems less like a hymn to brotherhood now than a sentence of bacterial doom. This generation of middle-class gay men stumbled into something it never dreamt of—this fever, these shakes. No helicopter can get us out of this one, I think as I sit watching them. From the window of this room, the helicopters don't so much symbolize the power of science as a desire to get away. Even the sick feel it, of course—most of all, no doubt. The Frenchman I know who stays in New York for his treatment says, "Now that I can no longer travel, I feel this huge nostalgia for Europe. If I could go anywhere now, I'd go to Greece."

How one must long to leave the tubes and catheters behind—the artificial parts—and go off to sunlit islands. Instead one stays and goes to yet another doctor. The Frenchman who dreams of Greece now takes a cab several times a week between two doctors in midtown who do not know about each other, so that he can qualify for the studies in which each one has enrolled him. Meanwhile everyone else eats out in restaurants, doubles his workload, takes trips to places he's always wanted to see with the unspoken thought: *I'll just keep moving till I have to stop. Who knows how much time I have?* New York is more than ever a study in contrasts. One goes from the hospital room to the ballet, from the restaurant to the friend battling with cytomegalovirus for his eyesight. One comes to New York—to its money, energy, modernity, sophistication—to learn what people are doing *now*. What they are doing now is lying in this room, as cold as a man abandoned on an ice floe in the Bering Straits.

Little Boats

OUTSIDE THE MUSEUM the *New York Post* shrieks, MAN SHOOTS GIRLFRIEND SAYS SHE GAVE HIM AIDS, furnishing enough scandal to get the office workers home from Manhattan to Queens on the subway; inside the Metropolitan Museum, a marmoreal murmur fills the entrance hall, and I decide not to check my coat. On this early November afternoon, I have walked up to the Met from St. Marks Place to clear my head. Halfway between the two, the public library is flying a flag advertising *Ten Centuries of Spanish Books,* one of which is the diary of Christopher Columbus, turned to a page written on his way to the New World the *New York Post* is now part of. (Did he think that it would lead to this? I wondered, gazing at his handwriting through the glass case.) The diary only put me deeper in the mood that brought me to the museum today: the desire to take a breath in some century other than this one. That's what a museum provides. I've come to this one at very different moments of my life: as a student, as a tourist, as a grown-up New Yorker who wanted to show his boyfriend the Christmas crèche. In the seventies it was perfect for a hangover, cool and quiet; after I stopped going out, I would come here because there was nothing else to do on Sunday morning.

Sunday, in those days, began at four in the afternoon—you could not call anyone before then. So when I started rising early I would have to find something to do. After killing time looking at paintings in the Metropolitan, I would go to the pay phone and dial the number of a friend who lived a few blocks away. My first question was always, "How was the music? Who was there? Did you get laid?" (*Art calling Life!*) Then, if it was okay to visit, I would run down the steps of the museum into the cold, exhilarating air of winter, knowing that when I got to my friend's I would very likely find, in his apartment, live originals of the faces I'd been examining in the silver light of the museum— especially the portraits on wood of Egyptian men of the Hellenistic Age in a small room just off the entrance hall, men with black eyes and black beards who uncannily resembled my favorite faces on the dance floor at Flamingo, when I was still going there.

Now the image of the handsome man has changed—he's blond, clean-shaven, Anglo Saxon, Calvin Klein'd—but in the seventies those Egyptians with black beards and eyes were so like the men I'd seen in bars and baths, they provided the same eerie sensation of staring across an abyss of time that I'd felt looking at the diary of Christopher Columbus—a chasm only objects, not people, can cross.

   Objects are what this place enshrines: so many, that walking through the rooms of armor, chalices, furniture, and paintings— the rooms of rooms—I think of some Henry James novel in which the contents of a house, the possessions of millionaires, are the goal of the protagonists, and the people themselves ephemeral. Museums are morgues, a friend of mine said once when he refused an invitation to come with me to this one; mausoleums in which plutocrats leave the booty they amassed during lifetimes on Wall Street, attempts, Freud said, of guilty businessmen to turn money (or shit) into Art. My friend's right, but although I understand what he meant, I never felt that way to the point of not going. I've always loved coming here. Even when I was happier in the Rambles than I was inside this building, I would still stop in the Metropolitan. Even when a man on a rock in Central Park was more compelling than one on canvas; even when it made me angry that the museum got permission to expand backward into the park and gobble up several acres of green, to make room for, among other things, the dining room of a stockbroker hung with El Grecos, I kept coming—though the Metropolitan, it seemed to me, was big enough already, and suffered from the same elephantiasis that homosexual life in the seventies seemed to exhibit, with its bars, baths, gyms, discos, mobs of men. By the end of the seventies it felt like there was too much of everything—so to get through either one, gay life or the Metropolitan, to maintain one's identity in this sea of muchness, I resigned myself to singling out a few favorite icons for which I reserved my admiration. Just the way we make a special place, in a museum like the Met, for a single cameo, a few paintings, some fragments of a torso, or a chalice, so I reserved my ultimate admiration for certain individuals in that mob of men on the dance floor at Flamingo.

Some of the homosexual icons are now dead, but in the museum the artifacts remain perfectly intact in its controlled light, humidity, and temperature. One of the great appeals of Art is that it has a very long shelf life. That's why I'm here. Everything has been so bad lately, I've come full circle: The student who abandoned Art after he discovered Life has had enough of Life for the moment. The man who preferred to spend his afternoon cruising the Rambles now wants the company of the inanimate. Back and forth we go. Last evening at the Jewel I looked at images of the nude male on its movie screen, and today I'm spending the afternoon looking at more male bodies in oil paint and stone.

There are too many, of course, but I have never been quite so open to them all as I am now. In the first room I enter, a curator and a preparator are hanging a painting from the Middle Ages. The curator stands back to see if it is crooked, directs his helper to pull the rope so that the painting rises on the left, and says, "I think that's right." Once, serving drinks at a party in a gallery, I bumped into a Monet. The host laughed at my chagrin, readjusted the painting, and said, "So much for the grandeur of Art." Paintings, after all, are just things hung on walls, but at the Metropolitan, in the silver light, they seem like religious objects. Many are. I walk through the rooms filled with images of gods and goddesses, Christ and the saints, heroes from the Bible. If you stop in a church on Fifth Avenue these days, you are often completely alone; you can sit there in a pew and rest, one thick door away from the hustle of the city. With the passing of the Age of Faith, more people come to *this* temple than all the others dotting Fifth Avenue all the way down to Washington Square. We no longer cherish God to the degree we cherish our artifacts, ceremonies, myths, and treasures. God is dead, Vermeer lives. This is known as humanism, and it makes Fundamentalists gnash their teeth. Yet today this museum feels like a refuge, a cathedral in a land of violence, as I walk through the clean, well-lighted rooms, past innumerable Christs on the Cross, and Holy Mothers, on my way to the newest thing, the American Wing.

The American Wing is part of that structure that gobbled up the green grass of the park and now regards the remnant apple trees as a vast, smooth wall of masonry on which tiny sprigs of ivy will be busy the next forty years climbing their way to the top— like so much else in Manhattan. For what? Looking at the American paintings in the new wing, they seem to me as lonely and isolated as I feel at the moment. Even the Winslow Homer of boys playing crack-the-whip in a meadow in New England looks far more austere and cold than the image reproduced in art books. There it has a Norman Rockwell quality, here the light on the meadow is thin and anemic. One can feel the chill of the pale air, the stony high-minded sobriety of New Hampshire, of cold floors on winter mornings. Several more paintings by Homer of waves crashing on gray rocks; landscapes by the Hudson River Valley School; and portraits—from colonial times to John Singer Sargents—deepen this sense of solitude. Only Eakins shows the naked body, but with the same light that's in Homer's

New England meadow. Santayana said life in America reminded him of the New Haven YMCA: sober, Christian, devoted to self-improvement. We were Puritan till very recently. Now we've been told it's our right to take a winter vacation and to find our G-spot. At the baths in Berlin last year I saw, on the screen of the TV in my room, forty nude Californians surround a swimming pool in a daisy chain, a Busby Berkeley homage to fellatio. Maybe the real American contribution to civilization, the last refuge of the male nude, is pornography. It is somehow the flip side of these sober paintings. We have always been two countries—Puritan and Cavalier—as there are two cities in New York right now: the infected and uninfected. One country is chaotic—illegal immigrants, heart transplants, pornography and drugs, homosexuals and AIDS. The other has been around much longer, and speaks from these paintings. Nothing decorative, nothing baroque. No crosses, and no Virgin Marys. No birth, and no death. Just the trackless forest, the mountain pass, the shaft of sunlight landing on a clearing in the valley, the solitary sitter. The New England soul Hawthorne and James described. The preexisting bedrock, as hard and gray as the Maine shore that Homer's waves crash upon. The country that sits and watches all the changes but does not really change, approve, or like them. In Santayana's novel *The Last Puritan*, two men are contrasted: The Italian is the happy connoisseur of life's pleasures; the American is a moralist too finely constituted to flourish, an idealist estranged from this earth. I think of them as I leave the forlorn light of the American Wing and walk back into the flowers, white arms, breastplates, helmets, velvet, and gold of Europe. The people, one feels, in the European rooms are not lonely.

My first year in New York I came here often to see a painting called *The Forge of Vulcan* for the smithy's graceful body and muscular back. There was a correspondence then between the faces and bodies in the paintings and those on the subway. They were connected, the men on their bunks at the baths and the gods depicted by Velázquez and Titian. There is nothing, of course, so voluptuous as a naked body in the American Wing. Only Eakins, who was fired from the art academy in Philadelphia for exposing the women in his life class to the pelvis of a male model, painted the nude—and then under the guise of boxers, athletes, young men at a swimming hole—that lonely, virtuous, Arcadian swimming hole! When an antisexual society decides to have sex, does it cease being antisexual? No. There was something compulsive, frantic, competitive in our quest for transcendent sex—Ahab in search of Moby Dick. Today the museum is full of youths staring, like deer in a forest, as they press the buttons on the tape machines that begin the recorded tour: American originals who wander somnambulistically through the rooms looking as forlorn, as scrubbed, as the boys playing crack-the-whip in that adamantine meadow. Their youth, their innocence, their health depress me in some way, since I came here today in part because a friend who stopped having sex nearly four years ago—in order to save himself—just got pneumonia.

In the next room two middle-aged couples sit together on a bench in front of an El Greco. One man says to the others, "You know, a lot of Jews went to Portugal when they were expelled from Spain, and they just converted. So there are a lot of Jews in Portugal no one knows about." *Who's counting?* I think. *They are.* Jews worry about Jews, homosexuals about homosexuals. Everyone else is largely indifferent to both. AIDS in America belongs to gays. That people care about the number of Jews in Portugal seems minor to me today; that youth has been sent to gape dutifully at the great works of art equally remote. I am looking for something I cannot find in either the American or the European rooms, and that is why I walk out of them to the top of the main staircase, turn right, and enter a room few people are ever in.

"They did *nothing* but make vases!" a German friend said one day, exasperated, when we entered this gallery. "In Berlin they store them in bomb shelters!" They do seem alike. Perhaps it is the monotony, the apparent sameness of the Greek vases, that numbs the viewer, for the same reason a crowd of men at Tea Dance leaves one blank: They cancel each other out. Reproduced in great numbers, even the beautiful item is meaningless. All the vases are of the same color, and, with variations, the same shapes; there is even a large chart against the wall explaining the functions of each, like an exhibit illustrating the various coins of a foreign nation. I could not tell one from the others for years. Then the *New York Times* carried a story one day about the acquisition of a vase depicting the death of Sarpedon; and a friend told me about Leagros. That was enough. When it seemed to me that the crowds at Flamingo, with their redundant physiques, were missing the point—when the tambourines and ethyl chloride, the rites of Tea Dance, seemed as suffocating as any law prohibiting sodomy—I would come into this pale room whose wooden floor creaks, and go to the glass case that holds a vase depicting the death of a warrior in the Trojan War. There, above the frieze of men in armor, the fallen hero with a wound in his side dripping blood, is an inscription in Greek that says, *Leagros is fair*. It is a mash note written to a youth the artist admired. We have been around a long, long time.

Bitter, dusty death—the death Homer speaks of so frequently in *The Iliad*, the death that comes to men so pitilessly—lies just beneath the words of praise. The death that does not figure in the American Wing, or even much in the European rooms, but which is so strong a presence in ancient civilization that when I leave the Greek vases I realize what it is I have come here for, and go downstairs to the room beneath this one that contains statues of Greek gods and athletes: the stone torsos whose beauty is so direct, so naked, I feel, at some level, embarrassed to look at them and always flush despite myself on entering the room. So undisguised is their celebration of the male form, they make me—covered in clothes, disguised in an age that makes my admiration guilty and concupiscent—uncomfortable. Their beauty stares the starer down. In life we try to possess it in the flesh; reproduce it in our gyms; ignore it with so much trivia—so much talk, and partying, and going back and forth—but here it is in its elemental form, freed of the decay of the flesh, the nonsense of daily life. Along the wall are glass cases containing objects the Etruscans made for people in the next world—a world we do not much believe in anymore—including a tray of food not unlike the one we could pick up in the museum cafeteria today. The stone torsos, the Etruscan chariot, a pair of Hispanic guards talking about their weekend, are at my back. But as I stare at the funeral artifacts, it seems to me this room contains only two elements: Beauty and Death. No castles, flowers, tunics, breviaries. Just The

Nude and The Netherworld. I cross the hall, through the tourists buying postcards, the roar of an enormous train station, and go into the Egyptian wing.

The Egyptian things all have to do with the netherworld. The Egyptians, we're told, put Death at the center of life; and we— who do not—have put on display the models of houses, cattle, servants, and boats they made for the tombs of men who owned such things in life. Against one wall I can still greet the gaze of those handsome men of the Hellenistic Age who resemble the men I saw Saturday nights on the floor at Flamingo. (I too live in a Hellenistic Age—half my friends I call "Helen"—an age, said Kierkegaard, when everyone goes about his business, believing in nothing.) Beneath the glass case in the middle of the floor I look down on the possessions of a rich Egyptian man, reproduced in miniature to keep their owner company during his residence in the next world. My favorite is the boat—little only in relation to a real one, floating down the Nile under sail and oar—made for a man who has died, the same way toys are made for small children to keep them company in their room at night, or food for a traveler to eat on a train. We do not make little boats. But then we do not really think there is an afterworld. The Egyptians considered death a journey; we think of it as disintegration. Thus—having disproved so many superstitions—we have stripped death not only of its mythology, but also of the comfort that mythology provided. The Egyptians had gods and goddesses. We have facts. Everything is chemistry. Somewhere between the Egyptians and us, Hamlet discovered the king could be used—after he dies—to plug a hole in the wall; and the afterworld became an undiscovered country from whose bourne no traveler returns.

And so, being unable to say with scientific certainty what's there, we tend to ignore it altogether. Not these people. The Greeks, the Etruscans, the Egyptians believed what Europe, upstairs, tried to forget, and America seems to have refused to contemplate: The Nude and The Netherworld.

It's five o'clock. Outside the sun has set. As I walk down the steps buttoning my coat, I feel the sharp stab of life that comes with the cold wind, the sight of the city after the museum. Welcome back to the world of fear and groaning, AIDS and the *New York Post,* doctors' offices and vials of blood. It is more shocking than leaving a church. Life, with its competition and decay, fills Fifth Avenue. I am supposed to telephone a friend who lives on the Lower East Side in a neighborhood populated by young men who resemble the portrait of Juan de Pareja in this museum. He has for the past few years been photographing them and has amassed a collection of his own that the museum is not interested in. Tonight Junior is coming over for a photographic session. I'm invited to watch. Strange. One used to sleep with Junior, but now you watch a friend take his picture. The whole city's a museum now. We're all voyeurs or exhibitionists. Once at this museum, I saw a fat man walking around the paintings with a beautiful youth in tow, and when I went down to the Club Baths later that evening, I passed a room whose door was open, looked in, and there they were: the fat man lying against the wall, an impresario displaying his concubine, a beauty whose bored air in the museum was replaced here by a sexual leer, full knowledge of his priapic power in this red-lighted chamber: Caravaggio with poppers. Tonight it is simply to be photographs. I reach the pay phone and dial the number. The trees of Central Park form a dark crosshatch against the pale orange sky. The wind is turning bitter. My friend does not answer. The museum behind me is closed by now, the city before me darkening as night falls. I hang up the phone and stand there, not knowing where to go.

Talking to O.

THE FIRST PLACE I saw O. was Central Park—one sunny
spring Sunday in the early seventies, after dancing all Saturday night, regrouping with friends the next day in an apartment
on Madison Avenue, and then strolling west. The drummers
were beating their bongos around Bethesda Fountain, the nan-
nies from Park Avenue were watching their boys push sailboats
across the pond, and clones were converging on the Rambles to
cruise, when O.'s retinue was spotted on the horizon of blossom-
ing apple trees. He was a man of medium height, with thick
black hair, black eyes, and black mustache—of Hungarian and
Turkish parentage. He spoke in a deep, resonant voice, slowly,
with a pronounced Turkish-British accent that was, depending
on his emphasis, capable of being either very funny or very serious. He had, even on a sunny Sunday in Central Park, surrounded by blossoms, a slightly melancholy, weary air—in those
dark eyes, in that rich voice, was a sense of the difficulties of life.

When he urged members of his entourage who split off that afternoon to go their separate ways to "Call me tomorrow, at the gallery!" "Don't forget Tuesday night, La Escuelita!" "Irene is coming to town on Wednesday, let's have dinner!" in each conventional exhortation there was an urgency, a seriousness, that might have characterized a father telling his child to watch out crossing the street and be home in time for dinner. This impression was not far off: O. had brought most of these people from a former life in London and ran a gallery with which several were connected—a gallery that sent O. traveling a lot. But when he was at home in New York, it was at his place that all of them got together.

Food was only part of it. An evening at O.'s involved, above all, conversation—with people one had never met: journalists from Athens, an artist from Mexico City, an old boyfriend of O.'s from Rome. His circle—a circle of friends so constant, so faithful, they had followed one another from city to city and constituted, more than any other I knew, a family—was fixed but fluid, loyal but independent, a function of O.'s affection most of all—his cooking, you might say. Most of them, including O., sold artifacts of one sort or another. But though the world that exchanges art for money is notorious for its meanness, O. was very kind. "Come on up, I am just back from Japan, I want to see you!" he said on the phone. And you went. O. included, invited, charmed, cooked for, and amused so many people that, going uptown to have dinner there, one always felt a bit like a child on Christmas morning—one never knew what would be under the tree.

He was the best of hosts—that's all. The Middle Eastern food, the stories about Cavafy, Japan, Lima, the candles, the beautiful room in a brownstone on the Upper West Side we gathered in, were a kind of rosy, glowing tent that O. had set up for his friends. And set up skillfully. Somewhere Santayana distinguishes the arts of poetry, music, painting from the arts of life; the latter are not monuments more lasting than bronze—they last the length of a dinner party—and yet they provide, really, in so many cases, what earthly happiness we have. O. was a master of these. O. embodied that Spanish proverb: "Living well is the best revenge." Once I ran into O. in the hallway of the St. Mark's Baths, shortly after I had published a book. I was standing in the stairwell of the third floor, brooding about the hopelessness of this cold feast of flesh we gay men had evolved as a way of life, when O. came out of someone's room, beaming. "I have just had a rather wonderful screw," he said, rolling the last R. I had not, and dumped on him all the reasons this bathhouse was cold, cruel, alienating, and depressing. O. listened and then said with the faintest smile, "Ah! So success has not made you happy." (Bingo.) His wit, however, did. O. saw things, but saw them without the slightest malice or reproach, so that even your own faults seemed merely human, and less important than the way in which they were phrased. Marriage, said George Bernard Shaw, is a long conversation—so, for that matter, is friendship.

Yet I don't suppose I spoke to O. more than once every three or four months; but when I did—bicycling out to Prospect Park or coming back from Jones Beach on the train—the pleasure was so rich that no matter what we were talking about (the Gulbenkian Museum in Lisbon, the latest sex club south of Fourteenth Street, mutual friends), I think of that decade in part as a conversation with O. And the spell of that spring Sunday in the park—those white apple trees—continued intact, enriched by the passing of time, in each encounter. After leaving Manhattan at the end of the decade, I realized, before very long, how much I missed our conversations, and O. became for me, every return visit, one of the people I could not wait to call. He acquired, in fact, for me, an ideal quality; because I saw him rarely, perhaps, or because he *was* rare, or because he lived in a world different from mine, he became a dream of New York. A dream of New York, dreamt down South, that was harder to square with reality each time I returned. For every time I returned, it seemed everything had changed, changed utterly; even conversations with friends—they, like everything else, sank inevitably beneath the weight of that subject that, though it came last, had banished all humor, liveliness, and joy.

The names of the dead, the shock at their number and improbability, the forecasts for the future, the dismal withdrawal and isolation, left one, in the end, speechless. Impotent. There was no way to leave friends in a glow of laughter or affection anymore; there was not even a moral to draw, or an interesting observation, because the plague, with its time lag, its scope, was revealing itself to be some sort of indiscriminate flu, leaving each person alone in a solitary confinement of fear. Conversation, like so much else in New York these past few years, was not much fun.

Perhaps that was why I called O. each time—O. was out of New York as much as he was in it and would be able to describe not only his trip to London, but place in context, perhaps, all that was happening here. "Are you in town?" he said one evening in 1985. "Come by and have supper with us!" Yet the park I walked across that twilight seemed deserted now—a few men sat on the usual benches in the Rambles, seemingly as ignorant as the rats scampering across the path in front of them. And when I got to O.'s, only three of us—O., his boyfriend, and I—sat down in a corner of that large white room, at a small table by the window, in a shrunken pool of lamplight; the rest of the apartment in shadow, like some house whose owners have died, and whose furniture is all under sheets. We ended up discussing, after the amusing topics (the topics that had formed, I realized now in retrospect, the entire menu of our lives), the gloom of the city. "Most of my friends," O. said in a weary voice, "are having trouble negotiating middle age." *What did he mean by this?* I wondered, even as I admired the expression. The city was so full of secrets now—a minefield, and we the mines—I could not be sure what he was referring to. I finally took it on its face: O. meant that the plague was not the only thing happening to New York. Time had passed, too, and even O. had a distinguished silver streak down one side of his thick black hair. AIDS and middle age were but two very different versions of the same thing: dying. The first beyond our power of comprehension, the second all too familiar. So this is what even O. has come to, I remember thinking: middle age. A few months later, I learned this remark was more subtle and detached than that, was only his dry and characteristic way of alluding to something I did not know at the time: While in Japan—fascinated, observant, doing business—he had discovered he had AIDS.

When I returned to New York that fall, I called O. from a pay phone on Thirty-fourth Street. It was the middle of an October afternoon; I gathered he was at home alone and asked if I could stop by. I wanted to see O. for several reasons: One, I always wanted to see him; two, I wanted to learn the stage of his illness; and three, I thought I'd better see him one more time—combining, in one uneasy mixture, the past, present, and future. The past: the good times, the happiness. The present: *How far along is he?* The future: *Why didn't you see him, tell him how you feel, let him know you care for him?* (A friend who runs errands, sleeps over, takes someone to the hospital, does not have to say this. Only those who don't wonder how they can.) The park was empty when I walked through it. I had been thinking since I heard the news I should write or phone O. about his diagnosis, but had been unable to find the words. And even now as I walked west, there seemed to be nothing to say that would sound right. I hoped in the act of visiting him that words would make themselves known. I rang the doorbell; the buzzer released the door; I went up the stairs, my heart accelerating not only with the climb; I heard a door open before I reached the top, and a moment later, there was O.—in his socks, looking much the same. We imagine from a distance all sorts of things. I walked in with the familiar pleasure of a child entering a chocolate shop—a place in which everything pleases—surviving even this, and we sat in the big white room and talked.

We talked about the novel he was reading that lay open on the table between us—a historical trilogy about the Balkans by a British writer. Then about mutual friends. And his trip to Tokyo. It was about the Japanese he talked at length in the way I loved: O. was such a good observer. He looked a bit haggard, but not much, and he still talked in the same calm, intelligent, vaguely melancholy, witty way. As he answered my questions about the Japanese, I felt that nothing had changed. Then I changed the topic.

And he answered my questions about his health. He discussed the doctors, pneumonia, reactions to medicine (including one that had made his skin peel off), inhalations, alternative therapies. *O.'s life is all doctors now,* I thought as I sat there, *all doctors and hospitals.* He talked about telling his mother. He wanted to visit her, but a doctor had said there was an association between jet travel and the onset of pneumonia in some patients. He had gone to an avant-garde Hungarian whose mixture of medicines had proved a mistake. He was now going to Sloan-Kettering to inhale a medicine that blocked the pneumonia. He stopped finally—after I, completely comfortable, marveling at his enabling me to feel this way, posed yet another question—and asked, "Is this an interview?" He smiled, enjoying the irony, and his eyes sparkled. I smiled, and said, "No." I wondered as we sat talking if I should, or could, tell O. how much I admired and liked him—but to do this seemed artificial and awkward. So I wondered if he knew without my saying so. And I began to think of Proust's aunts. In *Remembrance of Things Past,* the narrator's two aunts are so horrified by the idea of thanking Swann for the wine he brings them one day—thanking him in an obvious way, that is—that they ignore it altogether, until, shortly before Swann leaves, they slip in a reference to the gift so subtle that only the narrator realizes they are acknowledging the wine, so oblique that Swann leaves oblivious of their gratitude. I sat there thinking O. had given me wine, too—in this very room—a lot of wine, a lot of laughter, a lot of wit, conversation, happiness. But I could no more refer to it now than Proust's aunts could draw attention to Swann's present. Even worse, I didn't want to thank O. for giving me anything; I wanted to thank him for being.

(Including being himself, so wonderfully, now.) And there was certainly no way I could phrase that. So I left. I left O. twenty minutes before his own departure to visit a doctor and refused the tea he offered me, when he went to the stove to turn on the burner, thinking, *There is no need to stay with him. That would be too solicitous.* It was a gray, gloomy afternoon, not one that made being at home alone cheerful; but I was loath to do anything that gave the impression this was a visit in the slightest bit final. I walked down the stairs thinking it had been, after all, only another visit with O. The huge wooden door closed behind me, I left O.'s block refusing to think this might be our last conversation— who could? And what if? There was *still* nothing to say. And I walked east into the park that had been, fifteen years ago, the site of those strolls, those springs, those conversations whose jokes now seemed to have occurred in another language. This Sunday was overcast and gray, the trees still green, and entering this park with that sense of expansion and hope it always gives, I thought, *O. is putting on his coat now to visit the doctor, while I am walking into the park.* The sense of the unfairness of life was then replaced by a sense that I was being followed—by a lean, red-haired man, walking above me on the hill overlooking the Serpentine. I looked back, and we began to circle, like hawks on an air current. We met beneath a copper beech; we said nothing; I unbuttoned his shirt and ran my hands over his body; he turned away moments later and ejaculated into the air; zipped up, walked off, and disappeared from the park—without saying a word. All the way home the city seemed pervaded by silence.

Reading and Writing

Today the galleys of a book called *When Someone You Know Has AIDS* arrived. The book is addressed to two sorts of people: those with AIDS and those caring for people with AIDS. Since the line between these two categories is a thin and shifting one and merely the passage of time can put one on the other side of it, the book, like everything else about It, is something you grit your teeth to read, in order to prepare yourself for any new shocks. It would not be too much to suggest that much of a person's reaction to the subject of AIDS is directly related to his chances of getting it himself. If the man beside you at the lunch counter as you sip your soup can say vigorously, emphatically, "They should put them on an island and let 'em all die," that is because he has no fear of getting AIDS himself. The homosexual has no such option; he's part of it. What part he may not know. What part he may not want to know. But AIDS is not the only thing spread by a virus. Six years ago the media were so silent on the subject, gay men could not get the *New York Times* to even mention the fund-raiser they held at Madison Square Garden to raise money for AIDS research. (The same weekend a march up Fifth Avenue in support of Israel was also ignored by the paper; the following week, deluged with protests from both groups, the *Times* apologized in print to only one—it was not the homosexuals.) But now one can hardly pick up a newspaper or turn on the television without confronting the subject. Most of us have seen the statistics by now. Many of us have seen our generation wiped out in announcements from the Harvard School of Public Health. Some of us have been told we were terminally ill by Barbara Walters. Which is why one stops reading the stories finally, turns off the TV when the topic is introduced, or closes the galleys of books like the one that arrived this morning, wondering if—when dying—you will think, *Oh,* this *was covered in chapter six!* (As a friend said, "No one has to teach me how to die.") As admirable as the writing or publishing of books about AIDS may be, I really don't know who reads them with pleasure— because I suspect there is one thing and one thing only everyone wants to read, and that is the headline CURE FOUND.

Someone at the Whitman-Walker Clinic in Washington said that working with AIDS is like "staring at the sun"—so, in a way, is even reading about it. When the plague, or rather knowledge of the plague, appeared in New York several years ago, I remember hosts telling guests that they were not to talk about it at dinner. It spoiled the party. A few years later I was so worried that the subject would repel readers (I still assume this, since I, too, am a reader and that is my reaction) that I discussed it only when

I had to; eventually, just as the dictatorial cruelty of AIDS touched everything, it seemed I had to, all the time. But though I relieved my own anxiety and depression by writing about AIDS in these essays ("Do you feel a *duty* to write about AIDS?" asked a friend), I turned myself, as a reader, to pure escape.

That first summer I picked up a novel by Henry James I'd not finished years ago, *The Wings of the Dove*. It, too, was about death: the untimely death of someone young and fortunate. Then I read the life of Henry James himself, wondering how we had gone from his sense of Victorian repression ("Live, live all you can, it's a mistake not to!") to our present predicament. But his biography could not explain the appalling news on CBS.

Journalists, said Schopenhauer, are professional alarmists, but if their news was needlessly plunging people into gloom (a man in Italy who confused his flu with symptoms of AIDS shot himself, his wife, and his child; a friend in New York took an overdose for the same reason), the facts seemed for a long while to justify their headlines. That was so because, from the start, fact has far outstripped fiction in this matter. Fact has been, like the virus itself, something individuals and society have had to struggle to catch up with, in a state of shock. Writers who dealt with homosexual life before the plague—the manners and mores of the homosexual community—have been quite left behind by a change of circumstances that blew the roof off the house they had been living and writing in. A novel about AIDS was written early on called *Facing It*, but that was just what I didn't want to do; at least in literary terms. Novels weren't needed; one only had to read the series of interviews carried in the *Washington Blade* with a man named Engebretsen, who allowed a reporter to visit him periodically as he withered away. The truth was quite enough; there was no need to make it up. To attempt to imagine such scenes seemed impertinence of the worst kind.

Meanwhile the *New York Post* began to shriek lurid headlines that in more innocent times many of us had collected as High Camp: lovers jumping out of windows, hospital patients diving ten stories onto the sidewalk. The sexual practices of men who went to the Mineshaft were now known by married people who went home to Kew Gardens on the subway after a day spent working in Manhattan. Words and concepts previously thought too shocking to be mentioned came across the airwaves on National Public Radio, and I began to read books about other epochs in history when people had been subjected to cruel and unusual catastrophes. The Black Death was the most obvious; but when I looked at *The Decameron,* I saw the plague was merely the pretext for its storytellers to entertain each other with bawdy tales about ordinary life. So I turned to books on the French Revolution and the Terror (which is what most gay men in New York were going through at this time, exactly). The gouged eyeballs, footmen hacked to death in Marie Antoinette's bedchamber, beheadings in the Champs de Mars on guillotines that were, like AIDS, not always swift or instantaneous, seemed to match what we were being rapidly reintroduced to: the savagery of life. A savagery most Americans have always been spared. Then one evening I found an old issue of a *National Geographic* devoted to excavations at Herculaneum, the city destroyed along with Pompeii by the eruption of Vesuvius—and found the image I'd been searching for, in the skull of a woman with teeth clenched against the gas, pumice, ash suffocating her and her companions on a beach, as they tried to flee a city as helpless and startled and devastated as my own seemed to be. Disaster, real disaster, always comes as a shock.

A friend who was writing a novel on AIDS (it seemed inevitable there would be novels; indeed, most perversely of all, those being published that dealt with gay life, but did not deal with AIDS, were dismissed, reprimanded, for this fact) said he refused to write a "gloom and doom" book—but that was all there seemed to be around. Each time one tried to outline such a novel, one could not imagine the plot that would stand for, or include, all the stories one heard every day happening in reality to friends and their families in New York City and elsewhere— stories that broke the heart, if the heart was not anesthetized already. Writing about It, besides, presented an ethical dilemma: How could one write truthfully of the horror when part of one's audience was experiencing that horror? How to scare the uninfected without disheartening those who had everything to gain by cherishing as much hope and willpower as they could? "Don't you think it's time now," a friend said, "to introduce some light at the end of the tunnel?"

In those plays and films we had grown up with, of course it was, but when one sat down to think of some such illumination, there was nothing the *Times* had not done already in articles on AZT, or the galleys of the book that came today. Surely things had improved, in relative terms; one thinks still with pity of those friends who were the very first to get sick. Their dilemma and anger ("Why me?") were so awful; the first visit I made to a friend in the hospital convinced me, as I left his room, that the only moral thing to write now was comedy—anything to amuse, to distract, to bring a laugh, an escape from this dreary, relentless, surreal reality. But when it came time to make jokes, the air in which laughter thrives seemed to have dried up. How could one write comedy when the suffering was real? How could one write at all, in fact, when the only work that mattered was that of the men organizing social services, taking care of friends, trying to find a microbiological solution to a microbiological horror in laboratories we could not see? When World War I began, even Henry James abandoned fiction altogether—that huge edifice of prose, that elaborate manor house of tales and metaphors—and went to London to visit soldiers back from the front. (As had Whitman during the Civil War.)

And just as James realized that novels were beside the point, or were at least momentarily repudiated by the fantastic brutality of war, so now the act of writing seemed of no help whatsoever, for a simple reason: Writing could not produce a cure. That was all that mattered and all that anyone wanted. One couldn't, there-fore, write about It—and yet one couldn't not. A vast sense of impotence—the same helplessness the doctors were beginning to feel—spread over everything. The only conceivable function of writing about It seemed to be to relieve the writer's own anxiety and depression; but who needed that? The *Times* was now run-ning virtually an article a day about some aspect of the plague: its effect on the arts, its effect on doctors, its effect on fashion, its ef-fect, even, on the Pines. Films made for television, plays, and short stories began to appear. Publishers wanted a novel. The novel is occasionally the way we bring some sort of order to the disorder of life. But *this* disorder seemed way beyond the writer's powers. Literature could not heal or explain this catastrophe; the one thing about the plague that became clearer as it progressed was its senseless, accidental, capricious quality. This dumb virus killing the thing it fed on, destroying an organism infinitely more complex, advanced, skillful, *human* than it: Was there a lesson to be learned? Yes. That we live on a planet in which many forms of life still feed on each other. Beyond that—despite the vast "I told you so" of the Bible readers—there was nothing else to say. Not about homosexual life, certainly. If the homosexual lifestyle that had evolved before the plague was good or bad, contributed or did not contribute to human happiness, that was an issue to be addressed on its merits or lack of them. No one had led it, after all, in the light of the plague. No one expected it to charge that sort of price. The wider the field the plague moved across, the more unrelated its targets—nuns, babies, African heterosexuals, American homosexuals—the more meaningless it became. The plague may well turn out to be an irrelevance, an aberration, an interruption in the flow of history—a kind of fatal flu that had no more moral or metaphorical or social significance than the common cold. World War I, we say, had causes, meanings, lessons. The Spanish influenza, which carried off hundreds of thousands after the war, did not.

And yet because as long as it lasts, we must think of it as a war and not some fatal flu, writing about AIDS will appear, and in the short term will almost inevitably be judged, I suspect, as writing published in wartime is: by its effect on the people fighting—in other words, as propaganda, not art. Indeed, it will have to be about fighting—it must be in some way heartening— it must improve morale, for most people to allow it a place of honor. Otherwise they will dismiss it as useless, discouraging, immoral, like any art that accepts surrender during a war; even though the plague has in reality produced a deep depression—a depression that alternates between numbness and horror, fatigue and fear. For a certain segment of the American population, the plague has been a cram course in death.

For this very reason friends argue that gay life has come of age in dealing with all this suffering, that gay men and their relationships with one another have been changed forever. But I wonder. What is there to learn? A great many people lived a certain life that, within the bounds of what they knew at the time, was reasonably safe. But, like schoolchildren who learn years later that the school they attended was lined with asbestos; or like families who are told, twenty years after buying a house, that they live on a mountain of PCBs, the homosexuals who lived in New York, San Francisco, Los Angeles in the seventies, lived with a devotion to health and appearance that was part of their stereotype, learned afterward that all the while there was an invisible germ circulating in the fluids of their sexual partners that was capable of entering the body; of lying undiscovered, unnoticed, unseen for several years; and then of destroying the system of biological defenses by which humans have been able, through eons of evolution, to live on the planet. This plague was retroactive—and hence it seemed doubly meaningless, doubly unfair. It was so unfair that it belonged to that category of events—earthquakes, droughts, tidal waves, volcanic eruptions—that simply happen and that engender in those who survive nothing more than a reminder of how unstable a planet this is. Someday writing about this plague may be read with pleasure, by people for whom it is a distant catastrophe, but I suspect the best writing will be nothing more, nor less, than a lament: "We are to the gods as flies to wanton boys; they kill us for their sport." The only other possible enduring thing would be a simple list of names—of those who behaved well, and those who behaved badly, during a trying time.

Sheridan Square

I T'S LATE AUGUST, and Sheridan Square is mobbed. I'm not
sure what Sheridan Square is, exactly—the stretch of Seventh
Avenue that people cross at Christopher Street; the cement island
with the newspaper kiosk and subway entrance; or the triangular
park with the statue of General Sheridan in it, to the east of both.
Whether or not any of these is the actual "square," the two sides
of Seventh Avenue are so different that Christopher Street is obviously broken up by something. To the west of Seventh Avenue,
all the way to the river, the street that has given its name to a
magazine, a parade, a financial services company, and other busi-
nesses has been, for some time now, a busy, commercial, sometimes sleazy, public *paseo* of a sidewalk. The part of Christopher
Street east of Seventh Avenue that borders the park, however, has
always seemed to me one of the quietest oases in Manhattan.
Every time I enter it, walking west down Grove, or Christopher
Street itself, it looks to me like a little slice of Paris or London.

There's something dignified, quiet, and elegant about this pie-shaped patch of the city. And the park is what gives it this character; the park in which I have never stopped, until today.

The first thing I notice when I sit down—between a friend (on my left) and a beautiful stranger (on my right) who drunkenly asks if I've heard if the hurricane has hit Florida yet—are the statues; the gay "monument" whose installation was announced years ago and then postponed for some time. Long enough, at least, for us to stop thinking that these George Segal statues—of two men standing, two women seated on a bench—would ever be put up. But here they are. The sculpture group is not what you would call inspiring. In fact, one could write an essay on the change in values, style, mores, reflected in the contrast between General Sheridan on his stone pedestal and these four wan figures on the ground—but I'm glad it's here. The trouble is the figures look as if they are made of wet paper towels, and the expressions on the faces are so—expressionless. The men seem not very happy about meeting each other, or whatever they're supposed to be doing, and the women are positively stolid. Indeed, they seem deeply glum.

In contrast, the homosexual life around us is unbelievably kinetic—men of all ages, shapes, sizes, and fashion sense are crossing Seventh Avenue in the August sunlight, heading down Christopher or Washington Street. They don't see us. We sit inside the tiny park like divers in a cage, while everything else swims past, in this voyeur's paradise of a city. The people on the benches facing one another in the park are black and white, middle-aged and young, mostly male. To the left of the sculpture, two men in off-white clothes sit side by side—in color and expression, not unlike the statues—and every five minutes, another pair of gay men comes into the park to photograph each other, with one arm around the shoulder of the Segal sculpture: laughing, smiling tourists, apparently, making a photograph that will be an amusing record of their trip to Greenwich Village when they're back home (in Rio, or Jersey City). The sunlight dapples the ground. Cabs float past. The west end of the park narrows to an arched entrance covered in wisteria: very nineteenth-century, with connotations of a gazebo or a theater set. It couldn't be prettier. But the prettiest thing of all, the best part of it, is simply our ability to sit here, unmolested, or lie down in the case of my friend, for as long as we want. I'm relieved—because I don't know where to go next. As Hannah says in the movie *The Night of the Iguana*, "Oh God, please can't we stop now?"

We're stopped, all right. After an unnerving scene in a restaurant across the street, a little pub called the Lion's Head, just a few doors down from the original Stonewall Inn, the birthplace of it all—a pub, like this park, I've walked by a million times without ever stopping in, till today. It's my friend's condition that has brought us to both places: his manic desire to go out, even though he's anemic, has two T-cells, Kaposi's sarcoma lesions on his ear, chest, face, neck, and legs. He looks like a homeless person; he has all day, since I met him outside his hotel near the South Street Seaport, where he was lying in the sunlight on the sidewalk when I arrived. Instead of suggesting we move indoors, I sat down with him and learned, as we conversed, how easy it is in this city to live on the street. No one even glanced at us. Then we got in a cab and came up here, looking for a restaurant he could not find, till we simply had the driver stop and got out here: Sheridan Square. The place a gay man in New York in the seventies could always return to, the place a gay man felt he belonged, or at least could use to gather his thoughts and make phone calls till he found out where he was going next.

The Lion's Head was a discovery. The waiter was very considerate. Every place we've gone to eat—America, Spaghetteria—has been considerate. It's so obvious my friend has AIDS, you get a table real fast. If you want to be seated very quickly, take a Person With AIDS to dinner. Everybody's respectful. But it's been embarrassing, because Jeff has been behaving like a diva. He orders gazpacho, and pours his lime rickey into it to improve the taste, and then ends up putting his cigarette out in the bowl. Food is always ordered, and never eaten. He just wants to smoke. He calls for water, and then the check, in a peremptory, powerful voice that carries through the restaurant. The volume of his voice comes in surges; he starts in a normal tone, and then, if you try to speak, or he sees some potential opposition, or any reason whatsoever to speak loudly—such as the waiter standing a few tables away—the volume surges with alarming force, like something carried on an updraft, and becomes quite loud. All this is deeply embarrassing to someone brought up to be polite. And fascinating at the same time—because it's a scene. It's theatrical. It's sad. It's like going to a restaurant with Death in Ingmar Bergman's *The Seventh Seal.*

Now he's at rest—lying down on the bench, his skinny, skinny legs dotted with lesions, some of them covered by his Ralph Lauren shorts. Or are they Banana Republic? Whatever, he is, and has always been, the most acutely perceptive person I know on the subject of fashion, which he studied years ago at F.I.T., before going to work at Saks, before deciding he despised retail, before meeting a porn star/landscape gardener and moving to San Francisco, where he went to work for AT&T, and then, after the lover died, developed AIDS himself and came back east to be with his family. His arm lies across his eyes. His other hand is on his chest. On his legs are two large scabs where two lesions were lasered; on his hooded sweatshirt is the word COLUMBIA. The night before, at Spaghetteria, he put the hood on and ordered the waiter to turn down the air-conditioning because he had AIDS. Incredibly, in a restaurant filled with other people, the waiter complied. PWA power. It's still potent in New York. My friend's a sacred totem. He's also somewhat nuts. But then this city has had that on its streets for years and years now, and to its great credit, we can sit here in this park in perfect freedom.

Quelle collection: in this little park. I've been studying people on the subway this visit, wanting to go up to each one and say, "How did you get here? What section of what immigration law—what jet plane—when, and why, and where were you when you made the decision to come here?" We are beyond the United Colors of Benetton at this point. Which is more startling—the ubiquitous nightmare of AIDS, or the sense that the city is just a turnstile people rush through, to be succeeded by other groups? I sit, slack-jawed, *bouche bée*, at history's unfolding. Who'd have thought any of this in 1973? No wonder I *plotz* this afternoon, grateful to be sitting between my friend and the drunken beauty with the beer can in a brown bag in this park with its two monuments—one to the Civil War, one to gay people. Perhaps the George Segal sculpture makes sense in the end, because, amazingly, everyone on these two long benches is a George Segal sculpture. That's the point of a George Segal sculpture—and the history of art, and politics, for that matter: from the heroic, elevated (General Sheridan) to the mundane, pedestrian (the people on the benches). Just pour the plaster right over us. What the iron fence of this paved-and-planted triangle has momentarily captured from the city's teeming sea this afternoon would serve as a sculpture just as well. We're a collection ourselves, I'm thinking as I sit beside the friend I last shared New York with in the mid-seventies. Our friendship has a sort of epic sweep. The sort you find in thick paperback novels, or films like *The Way We Were*: individual fates worked out in a current of history that becomes apparent only after the lives are lived. Who'd have thought there would be a monument to gay people in Sheridan Square, and Jeff lying on a bench beside it covered with KS? I couldn't make this up in a novel, I think as I sit there. We're all that's left of a certain time; washed up in a park we never sat in all those years, grateful we can sit here now, out of the rushing stream, permitted, here in the heart of things, to be utterly out of it. Oh, the humanity of parks!

Or at least this particular enclosure. How many times, in a city so big, so gay, one never thought it needed a gay focal point, one has ended up here, after all. Here, where the Sheridan Square Gym used to float above Tiffany's, the coffee shop, not the jeweler, where one could eat beside a plate glass window and watch gay men go by beneath the weight-lifters who used to take their breaks between sets at the windows of the gym, their beefy, pumped-up arms on the windowsills, waving at their friends down below. Here, where the VD clinic used to be, where I learned, to my surprise, that I'd been exposed to hepatitis B. Here, where Charles Ludlam finally found a permanent theater—at One Sheridan Square—though the sliver of piazza immediately before it has been renamed in his honor. Here, where the Stonewall Riot occurred. Here, where George Whitmore, whose book about AIDS was called *Someone Was Here*, lived at Number Thirty-nine. Here, where the Oscar Wilde Memorial Bookstore has operated for years. Here, where a single street, Christopher, runs the gamut from the tony apartment building at the corner of Greenwich Avenue to the drag queens from the Bronx, and the AIDS hospice Bailey House, at the west end. Here, where it has all come down to these wan, dough-colored, expressionless zombies George Segal has made to commemorate gay men and women and their struggles.

Some struggles! I met Jeff when he was twenty-two, still a student at F.I.T., so young, with such high spirits, he seemed ready to pounce when he shook your hand. Even at the Tenth Floor, that tiny dance club where we met, there was an intense energy about him which found its minor expression in the way he walked, almost bouncing on the balls of his feet, and smoked one cigarette after another; a young man who loved fashion, nightclubs, and the serial romances he had with the older men he called Daddies. Jeff, who loved Fire Island and Flamingo, whose best friend used the computers of the law firm he worked for at night to compile a directory of men with big dicks in cities all across the country, a sort of Baedeker the two of them used when they traveled. Jeff, who finally moved to the gayest city of all, after he met the porn star/landscape gardener from San Francisco at a sex club off Tenth Avenue: a somber, almost religious place with long hallways of cubicles with communicating glory holes, where one night the porn star dropped his pants and revealed himself, Jeff said, to be "all dick." Jeff, the Irish American Catholic, who translated the devotion he'd felt as an altar boy to an adult preoccupation with the male form, and never lost his desire for ecstasy, transcendence. Jeff, who, when he said good-bye at the airport to the hot Italian he had ended up with in Connecticut, had gone into the men's room to stand beside him at the urinal and take one last look at each other's penis. Jeff, so health-conscious he would write paragraphs about the beneficial properties of broccoli in letters after he moved to San Francisco, letters that I had never been able to throw away because they were so full of hope and excitement and engagement with life, with their exclamation points and underlined words, their ten handwritten pages on a yellow legal pad, written when he was perpetually about to go out. Jeff, who was so aware of the importance of skin care he put cucumber slices over his eyes to banish wrinkles, who now lay beside me on a bench covered with purple spots, still full of some residue of nervous energy, essentially out of his mind.

The arm across his eyes is the most eloquent pose he could have adopted: the age-old gesture of a grief, or horror, beyond one's ability to comprehend. Outside the fence, on the other side of Jeff, I see a blond man with a crew cut who looks no more than twenty-five walking slowly down the sidewalk with a cane, in jeans and white T-shirt. He is very handsome. And, like Jeff, out on the street, despite everything. *Bravo*. Suddenly the beautiful drunk with the canal-green eyes lurches to his feet and walks out of the park, with his beer in a brown paper bag. Four queens get out of a cab. In a few hours people will be converging on The Monster. The friend who lives on this block, on Christopher Street, does not go out at all. He stopped looking several years ago. "Because I've *had* sex," he said, when I asked why. "Because what I want now isn't sex, it's emotional." Ah, I think, the old bugaboo—Loneliness—and the longing for Love: still so elusive after so many years of trudging this street. When they find the cure for AIDS, will they find the cure for that? Perhaps the reason the men and women in the George Segal sculpture look so bland, so lifeless, so wan, so blank, is that no sculpture could express that reality of gay life: its personal, emotional content. All that makes these figures homosexual is the fact that the men stand beside each other, and the women sit together. But what else could the sculptor have done? Shown them having sex? Exchanging phone numbers? Glancing back at one another over their shoulders? Taking a blood test? Easy enough to depict a general with a sword. Impossible to portray this other, different struggle—so unheroic, so isolating, so riddled with self-loathing and contempt. The irony of all the attention, the consideration, that gay people now receive—from the maître d' at America to the speeches at the Republican and Democratic conventions to this statue in Sheridan Square—is that most of it has come about at a horrible cost. All societies are founded on the blood of young men, wrote Oliver Wendell Holmes Jr. Assimilation, too.

The Names of Flowers

IT'S THE SORT of party I worked as a bartender my first few years in the city, and which I attend as a guest only a decade later. There's someone by the elevator with a list, checking names when I enter the building. There's a handsome young man in black tie running the elevator. There's a woman in a bathrobe, smelling of Pepsodent, who says she got stuck in the elevator between the basement and the first floor—a neighbor of my host. I never see her again, but the encounter with her in the elevator before I get off lessens the dread, when the elevator operator pulls back the metal grille and I step forward, of entering the loft filled with guests and waiters in black tie. The invitation said FOOD AND MUSIC. Hurrying downtown through deserted streets, later than I wished to be, I had visions of a concert one could not enter till the first movement was finished. It is much more chaotic than that. The thirty-five guests I imagined are one hundred thirty-five; the music can barely be heard; the room is roaring. It

is a cold April night. There are sprays of spring flowers throughout the room—more irises than I have ever seen at one time in a
cylindrical glass vase; strange lilies in a spotlight; flowers whose
names I do not know, which remind me of the Age of Parties—
there were always flowers whose names I did not know.

I don't imagine there has ever been a decade in New York when
people did not party; the paradox of New York is that this cold
northern city has always had the atmosphere we associate with
cities like New Orleans or Rio de Janeiro. I moved to New York
because of a party—the sight, from the balcony outside my room
on Fire Island Pines one summer weekend, of a Tea Dance on the
deck below: more good-looking men in one place than I'd ever
seen before—and the moment I arrived in town, I began going
out, first to the Loft, then the Tenth Floor, then to the parties given
by a friend on Madison Avenue, then to the theme balls given on
Fire Island in the summer, and then their continuation in town
in the winter, climaxing, for me, at any rate, in the Fellini Ball
staged by George Paul Rossel in the Rainbow Room. In the Age
of Parties, the invitations did not fit in the mailbox, and when
you opened them, glitter spilled out of the envelope; once it was
a poster by the artist Michaele Vollbracht. Eventually, the Black
Party and the White Party and the Star Wars Party and the
Magic, Fantasy and Dreams Ball all began to blur, and I wondered whether they were going to run out of themes. The world
was so small then that when I'd spot certain people on the street
in suits and ties, on their way to work, I would connect them instantly with a Roman gladiator, a headdress involving fruit, a
character from *La Dolce Vita*. And it seemed to me that the real

New York was this nocturnal colony of people who lived primarily to go to parties.

Of the people at the party in this loft I know the names of ten. They are clustered together in a corner beyond the table on which the glasses are lined up in neat rows beside the bottles and the waiters. I stand there on the edge of the room, looking at it like a man selecting a spot on a crowded beach before he puts his blanket and books down, and then I ask one of the two waiters at the long table for a drink. For a long time parties were more enjoyable to me when I worked them than when I came as a guest, but I've not been to a party of this sort in so long, or seen certain friends, that this evening is welcome. "No one has given a party like this in five years!" a friend said on the phone earlier that day. (Parties are like books, like plays: Occasionally the right one comes along at the right time.) This one's got everything: flowers whose names I have to ask, in thin spotlights; a quartet playing chamber music; waiters. It's as if the Age of Parties had been re-created—with one pleasant change: This one doesn't terrify. They used to. I used to attach myself like a leech to the only person I knew in the room—in the Age of Parties I only knew one—till he pried me loose with a lighted match and went off to talk, quite sensibly, to someone else, at which point I felt he had left me alone on a small ice floe, like Little Eva, in full view of the plantation owner's dogs. Now I can stand alone and survey the room before going over to join the group I know—mainly because there is a group I know. No need to panic (though some never did, were poised from the start). It strikes me as I pause there looking at the room, moreover, that this is something to look at a while longer; that what we once took for granted now seems extraordinary.

In the Age of Parties, there was always a single gladiolus under a pin light—like a photograph by Robert Mapplethorpe—because the Age of Parties—my Age of Parties—coincided with the seventies. The seventies produced a certain look. Sometimes it was called Industrial Chic. It was spare, modern, pared down, clean: the single gladiolus in a spotlight, a palette of grays and blacks, a loft in Soho or a new house in the Pines—they were all of a piece. Like the gay men who followed strict diets, exercised religiously, like dancers or athletes, and then on the weekends took enough drugs to kill a horse, the Age of Parties staged its fleshy bacchanals in rooms like this one, rooms you would have called minimalist. That was the look in art and the arts of life: flawless, clean, exact, controlled—so that the messiness of the sex that formed a petri dish in which HIV flourished seems to have been an escape from that life's discipline and deprivations. In the Age of Parties, the duality just got more and more intense: The torsos got leaner and tighter, while the parties (and eventually the dance clubs) got bigger and bigger, so that now, this party into which I am stepping seems like a mere shrunken remnant of an age gone by.

Even the friends who ten years ago did not know each other now do, and I tell myself to speak with the ones I see once a year, rather than those I saw the previous evening. Of course, it's still hard introducing oneself to strangers. But after many parties one learns there is nothing sillier than the reprimand, once the door has shut behind you, that your life might have been different had you only had the nerve to introduce yourself to Him. Perhaps this time I can introduce myself to the one in the red bow tie: one of several faces I have seen for years but never spoken to, and which now surprise, reassure, and comfort me because they are still alive. This is no small achievement in New York in 1985. Life here has assumed the suspense of a summer Sunday's tea dance—you're not sure who is going to disappear on the next boat. In this loft once lived a man who died at home, in complete secrecy, where now more than a hundred people go on with the next installment of the soap opera. He is in some sense still here. He was a handsome, kind, witty man who came to New York from Boston, a famous university, a close-knit family, to write about and live a homosexual life—and he collided with the thing that no artist's dream ever included. It was thought this might be a memorial service, but I learn instead it is a birthday, and the message of the party seems to be: Life goes on, with lots of irises. This seems obvious but is not. I spot an old friend across the room and wonder if I should say hello—because I've not seen him since the mutual friend died. I do, and we don't dwell long on the fact. The people who have introduced new mourning customs—replaced wakes with dinner parties at which slides of Fire Island are shown—refuse to give death more than its due. They refuse to be lugubrious. They refuse to be stupid, too, for the most part—and if before the hidden agenda of these gatherings was the pursuit of sex, now it is the avoidance of it. As a friend said, "No one in New York is having much sex anymore." This makes the party even more curious: An odd reticence pervades the room. What we are not speaking of we are not speaking of by mutual agreement. The collective ego has been dampened.

We're all afraid and grateful to be mobile and nervous because we can't say what the future holds. The curious thing is that, though one would think the decision that we are all so vulnerable would make us stay home and give up each other's company—the opposite is true: I enjoy more than ever the sight of homosexuals together. And if a way of life that was once high-spirited, hilarious, is now restrained, solicitous (as if someone went from adolescence to late middle age without the intervening gradations)—we are therefore more grateful for the party. Its taste and generosity and style remind us: Life was once like this. We talk about everything but It. And instead of asking what someone does in bed, we inquire, "Will there be chocolate for dessert?"

Looking at some of the guests I can tell which ones are celibate; which ones are having less, more cautious sex; and which ones are going right on with the old ways. It has nothing to do with one's degree of personal exposure to the dying; it has to do with temperament, with the way different minds respond to the same facts. We face each other, after all, over freshly dug graves. There are ghosts among us. We're the actresses who meet in the ruined theater in *Follies*. We're tourists who have been admitted to an exhibit of our own former lives. Here are the flowers, the lights, the faces—just as they used to be, when everyone was sleeping with one another. What fun that was. Watching *The Normal Heart* the previous evening, I stared—across the stage between my seat and those opposite—at a handsome man in a long-sleeved, button-down, neatly pressed shirt. He had thick, dark hair; a mustache; watchful, dark eyes; and—beneath his clean clothes— one of those substantial bodies whose broad shoulders, swelling thighs, represent meat, flesh, life. *"Stop screwing!"* the doctor on stage was telling the hero. *"Until this is over!"* And I looked at the man in the first row in the button-down shirt, as if at an éclair on the bakery shelf, and thought, *"Someday, when this is over, perhaps I can have just . . . one . . . more . . . of those."*

That's because there seems to be a lull on this spring evening—which, in this room full of flowers and handsome men, encourages fantasy. Someday life will be as it was again. In fact, on the surface of this city it seems exactly the same. In the past few days I have spent an afternoon in Central Park; seen the Caravaggios at the Metropolitan, the Mayan artifacts at the Museum of Natural History, *The Normal Heart* and *Parsifal* (two works with, strangely, a common theme); had lunch with friends on Second Avenue; watched men meet in my local park at night and leave together; even visited the baths and seen men too numerous to count. Anyone would say nothing has changed. The city goes on: The baths and bars and parks are busy. But there is another city. The doppelgänger that coexists with us: Invisible, mental, it draws attention to itself when I pass certain apartment buildings, a bathhouse that has closed, or enter a room in which someone used to live. So if this party seems to re-create a former life—whose felicities we took for granted—there is a mood in the room, the same sentimental delicacy two lovers feel who haven't seen each other in five years but meet in a restaurant they first went to every night the first month of their affair. It's not just that, as another friend said, "New Yorkers have a solution for every dilemma. But not this one." It's that what has happened has left its mark. What has happened to us in New York the past five years has made those who still remain *careful* with each other in a way they weren't before—almost tender. Gone is the old, caustic gossip, the sexual current that lay beneath a party like this to such a degree that reaching for an hors d'oeuvre, you were always wondering, *Who's in the bathroom now, and how long have they been in there?*

That's all passé—and in its place is a new reserve based on the simple truth that everyone has adjusted to new facts. Each one of us is Diseased Meat. Diseased Meat is blue-green; it stinks. It makes us think we shouldn't sleep with the man in the red bow tie even if we meet him. Now, there's Clorox and Oxynol-9 and hydrogen peroxide and condoms, and mutual masturbation at ten paces, but that's not what meeting someone in the Age of Parties led to. That's why the Age of Parties ended. That's why it took at least five years for the enormous impetus—the assumptions, standards, freedom, egotism—of Promiscuity, Inc., to slow. The men—who used to be hors d'oeuvres—are no longer edible. So the real hors d'oeuvres become the focus of our mouths. We praise the food, we talk about someone's student days in Paris in the *pissoirs* that are no longer there, and finally, the cakes on the table lined with bowls of strawberries.

And I think of a novel I've been reading by Henry James—a novel in which the heroine dies of an unnamed illness when she is still young, and her life is all before her. The model for this character, it's said, was James's cousin, who died of the disease that in the previous century eclipsed lives before they had run their course or achieved their purpose: tuberculosis. Her death haunted James all his life. The death of people before their time often does. The young writer who lived here had his career still before him; we will never know what he might have written. But it seems to me he was following the advice the doctor gives the heroine of *The Wings of the Dove:* "You must be happy. Any way you can!" How ironic! As I look out over the room at the guests, the flowers, the food assembled by a host who brought to his dead lover's illness the same tact and imagination he has shown in re-creating the Age of Parties, I remember something else from *Wings of the Dove*—the very last lines. As the quartet saws away at its instruments in the flower-banked corner, I think of the two lovers who meet each other in the final scene of the book and realize their plan to defraud the heroine of her millions has failed in a way that not only turns their world upside down but introduces a certain estrangement between them. "I'll marry you, mind you," says the man in an attempt to reassure the woman, "in an hour."

"As we were?" she says.

"As we were," he says.

And then: "We shall never," she says, "be again as we were!"

That's kind of it. And with this I walk across the room to find my host, whom I half hope not to find, since the right mixture of condolences and gratitude—the referring, or not referring, to the person he's lost; the thank-you for his party—is still not one I've grasped. The room is so crowded I give up with a good conscience. The man in the red bow tie gives me that blank look that seems to convey the sense that men are as nameless and perishable as the flowers I will not learn the names of tonight, either. The tall windows of the loft gaze down on the cold, empty street outside: the street that can no longer promise, when you leave the party, a man to sleep with, in place of the one you did not have the nerve to introduce yourself to here. In the Age of Parties there were lots of substitutes. As I go to the coatroom the refrain of a song that's been going through my mind since this began repeats itself: "The Party's Over." But is that right? It goes on behind me with laughter and talk and introductions, louder than ever. Perhaps everything *but* the party's over.

Ties

THE EVENING OF December 3, 1983, it rained hard in Manhattan, and yet I couldn't stay in my apartment—I had been living in a house in the suburbs all fall, where one stays indoors and things come to you (United Parcel, mailmen, relatives with day-old doughnuts). The chance to be out walking through the streets was intoxicating, even in the rain, even at the end of a rotten year, in the early-winter darkness. The year 1983 seemed to be a year of blows: the circumstances compelling me to leave town in September and now the funeral of a friend dead of AIDS that brought me back. If—before I left—I was like most residents of Manhattan, who lead, despite the cliché, lives as routine as people in small towns, I now found myself walking east from the Astor Place subway at five o'clock with the surge of adrenaline that affects tourists and the happiness of a traveler finally returning home. Home was the little hole-in-the-wall that sells Middle Eastern food to go, which was the first thing that brought me to a halt

near the corner of St. Marks Place and Third Avenue. Waiting for
the Arab to finish stuffing the pita bread for the woman on my
left, things looked the way they did to Emily in *Our Town* when
she comes back to earth as a ghost because she misses her old life:
Everything was poignant, as I waited for the Arab to toast my pita.
An actor from the Negro Ensemble Company came up and said
to the woman standing next to me that he'd been assured he
would be in the production they had just auditioned for, and as
they talked happy actors' talk, I thought, *Isn't this just how someone
imagines New York? You wait for the Arab to give you your pita sandwich while two ecstatic young actors talk about their next show, while
beyond the awning the rain is streaming down in slanting orange lines
and all these people are coming home from their day uptown to romantic little apartments in the East Village.* Was this rain real? Or
were we shooting a film? There was a functioning dry telephone in
my apartment just a few doors away, but the street, the crowds,
the excitement of being here again were so intense I went next
to the bank of pay phones near Second Avenue and started making my calls there. The handsome man who came up to use the
phone on my left intensified the romantic element—Who is he?
Who's he calling?—as the faces went past in the rain and I found
myself listening, in a few seconds, to a friend tell me he'd quit his
job in August, gone to Greece and Paris, nursed his lover through
hepatitis, changed his apartment, and wanted me to come to dinner that evening to meet the young man his roommate was "inter-
viewing" as a possible boyfriend.

When you leave New York and come back, the joke is you find
nothing has changed—despite the infinite number of trivial

events—but this time I learned a lot had: Not only had friends left their jobs or moved to new apartments, but most of them were depressed—one newly macrobiotic and saintly; another living half of each week in the country; another visiting doctors who told him to calm down; another who was asked to come back for a blood test. Returning after four months, I was like the relative of a patient recuperating in a hospital, or a parent who visits his child in school infrequently: One arrives and expects to see progress. You want to see your patient better, walking again, your child fluent in French, your city cured of the plague. But apparently there is no cure for this plague. There are things being tried—so many that one man who died said before he went, "The treatment is worse than the disease"—but the friend whose funeral I was here to attend had tried most of them. For that was why I was back—to attend the funeral of Eddie, a friend so bound up with New York it was hard to imagine the city without him, a friend who so unfailingly enjoyed everything that was new in New York—from nightclubs to phone systems to winter coats—even now I had the impression he'd got AIDS only because he was always the first to do everything.

Eddie's motto, in fact, if he had one, was that of Auntie Mame, his favorite heroine: "Life is a banquet, and most poor fools are starving to death." Not Eddie. Long past the point at which most people I knew had begun to slow down—to stay home on Saturday nights with Sunday's *New York Times,* to stop going to Fire Island, to stop dancing (unless it was what one friend replied when I asked him where he was dancing these days: "In my living room!"), to stop going out to new clubs ("I've been to all the nightclubs," one said, "including the ones that haven't opened yet"), to stop participating in the sixty things each night that made living in Manhattan distinct from living in, say, Rutland, Vermont—Eddie kept going. Eddie was out every night. He was in fact whatever you call the man who stands in front of certain nightclubs and decides who will get in and who won't. His life was nocturnal—he got home around four or five in the morning and then, if he hadn't arranged to have one of the bouncers from Brooklyn come over ("Let me put it this way—he has no neck"), he slept. For only four or five hours; like Napoleon, Eddie got by on less than most of us need. And then, from the depths of that eccentric apartment we'd christened the Eighth Wonder of the World, he awoke and began to telephone; depositing the details of the night before, the incidents, the shoes, the faces, the celebrities, into my ear as if I were the diary he was too busy, too excited, to keep.

He knew where to go in the East Village for a shiatsu massage, and where to go near Times Square for male strip shows, and where to go on lower Broadway for the cowboy boots and shirts he began buying after he and a friend returned from the gay rodeo in Reno. He had a pass to Man's Country—the baths we both frequented—and passes to three or four fashion shows a day when the collections were being shown. His dream was to go around the world on the *QE2* as a member of the crew assigned to dine and dance with widows from Omaha traveling alone. Instead he went to the dentist one day and learned he had tumors on his gums—tumors he showed me one day when they were larger and we were walking down Fifth Avenue in the bright sun-

light on our way to go shopping. "Do you want to see them?" he
said and then pulled his upper lip back so they were visible: dark
purple, like clusters of grapes.

Eddie was not embarrassed by anything personal; he began to
tell the people he met, "I have cancer, but I'm not going to die,"
in the same breathless, dramatic voice he used to describe the arrival of the king of Spain at Studio 54. And he telephoned every
morning with the same cheer to tell me not only that he'd fainted
in the hospital elevator the previous afternoon but that "that gorgeous boy we used to say had a Very Important Stomach—the
one who plays *baseball,* you know—came to my interferon group
today, only they gave him too much and he was shaking like a
windshield wiper. Covered with spots!" Eddie's spots went away
when he was radiated; then they came back; still, we listened to
the progress of his illness with a certain impatience, a certain re-
fusal to take it in—like children who cannot allow a parent to get
sick. Eddie, after all, was the central figure in our family of
friends—New York itself, somehow. When a man got on the elevator we were riding in one afternoon at the D&D Building and
asked politely, "How are you?" and Eddie said, "I have cancer,"
another friend of ours turned to Eddie after the man—speechless,
shocked—got off at the next floor and said, "Couldn't you say
you've been swimming *laps?*" For we somehow could not permit
him to be ill. And that was the only change in Eddie's appearance
we could see: a certain gauntness. Eddie claimed, "It's in the eyes.
I can tell, in any crowd, at any party, who has It. It's in the
eyes." And so, just the way he'd told us about Los Angeles—how
they dressed, what the houses were like—and the rodeo in Reno,

the crowd at Studio, the models in Kenzo's fashion show, so Eddie became the first traveler to a new and scary destination.

There was a white high-rise building about halfway between Eddie's apartment on Fifth Avenue and mine in the East Village—a building occupied primarily, it seemed, by elderly Jewish men and women who were often being wheeled up and down the sidewalk by maids from the Caribbean when I walked by. Across the street from them was a small school playground behind a chicken-wire fence and a churchyard in which apple trees bloomed in spring. I left New York not long after Eddie began treatments for his tumors; he would, with the enthusiasm and interest he had shown all his life for what was new and experimental, try anything—things we learned later had probably hastened his death. The next time I came back to New York on a visit, Eddie looked like one of the eighty-year-old Jewish men watching the children play kickball from his wheelchair across the street. He was dressed in a black overcoat and scarf, though it was a warm spring day; his face was even gaunter, and the flesh around his mouth seemed to protrude to make room for the tumors; he shuffled along at the pace very old people, who are usually in a wheelchair, use. We walked from the lunch he served at his apartment—he loved to cook for his friends, and only afterward did we learn he was careless about what he himself ate—to a store on University Place that rented videocassettes. He was bringing some movies back and he did so very slowly. He rented both conventional and pornographic films, and he took me to the shelves of cassettes to tell me which ones he'd rented ("*Teen Marine* is fabulous!") and select new ones. When he was shuffling out of the store, the people behind us finally could wait no longer and veered around him, like cars passing on a highway. Eddie only smiled as I waited on the sidewalk outside for him to finally cross the threshold. Smiled at their impatience, his own predicament. We parted on that corner; I thanked him for lunch and did not look back till I had crossed the street—to see him standing there, turning north to start his long shuffle back to his apartment, a man of forty in a heavy black overcoat and scarf on a warm spring day who happened to look ninety-five.

The friends whose mascot he had always been were faithful to him; one gave me news on the phone of how he was doing—the naps he took every day at five, a sudden blindness, his discovery of classical music. *Teen Marine* was beyond him now. He began listening to Mozart. That was how I—five hundred miles to the west that winter, taking a walk each night in the only place available, a local cemetery illumined by the lights of a nearby shopping mall—thought of Eddie: lying in the Eighth Wonder, blind, listening to Mozart. One Saturday morning the word came that relieved the strain, the knowledge of his suffering and the suffering itself. "Some private-duty nurse they hired called his brother at four in the morning," said the friend. "She wanted to know where her check was, Eddie was dead. Can you believe it? Eddie's gone, dear. Eddie's gone. He took a left."

That was the problem, as I stood there now on the sidewalk of a city that seemed inseparable from his voice each morning on the phone. One might as well say New York was finished. In fact everything remained, just as I remembered it—even the baths on my block whose two slender black doors people were going in and out of as I stood there watching. "There's no reason to go to New York anymore," two British art critics said in an article I'd read on the plane about the fall season in various capitals, "now that sex and drugs are Out." Try telling New Yorkers that, I thought. Ah, New York! Ah, humanity! It is banal by now to say the whorehouses in Paris were never as busy as they were during the plague. But when I went into the baths to sit in the cafeteria for a while, before the wake began—it seemed the right restaurant, in this case—I watched men passing the doorway in their towels who looked exactly as they did before the world turned upside down. The music in fact was wonderfully familiar— a flawless blend of the best songs of the seventies that made me very sentimental; Eddie and I had danced to some of them. Listening to "You're My Peace of Mind" as the men walked by, I thought, *The faces, the music,* were *wondrous—still are—and the fact that some virus has insinuated itself into the collective bloodstream through the promiscuity that homosexual life evolved is a medical, not a moral, fact.*

Or was it? I wasn't sure. Eddie was dead either way, and I left the warm cafeteria and its amazing view without touching the men we used to gasp over together (the central expression of our friendship: the gasp) and walked down St. Marks Place to the funeral home. The funeral home was only a block from the baths. The men gathering at the chapel in their dark suits and ties were even handsomer than those I'd seen pass the cafeteria—men I was used to seeing in towels or bathing suits, or in beach clothes on a sunny boardwalk. The rabbi—a whirling dervish on the dance floor one summer—speaks of a special generation that is

being singled out, afflicted before its time. It seems wrong that
the pleasure we shared should lead to death—it seems out of proportion to the crime; but, then, this is a medical, not a moral
fact. I feel numb and unreal in the little chapel. I have not taken a
full breath since entering; the air is heavier here, oppressive,
weighty, and thick. This is not happening, I think. This is not the
reason we gather together. These are the people Eddie has adored
all these years—*adored* is the correct word. These are the people
whose beauty he praised, whose style he appreciated, whose ex-
ploits he followed, whose friend he finally became. These are the
men who—handsome, bright, successful, original—constituted
the glamour Eddie, and New York, was so fond of. They do not
gather together for this. They come together for parties, for
beaches, for dinner, for fun—for a song that Eddie used to drag
me out of the house to run down to the bar to hear. ("The one
where the violins keep going up, up, up!") But there is the casket
being wheeled down the aisle, through the dense, airless room.
There are Eddie's parents—this collision of Eddie's two worlds,
his past and his present—in the midst of these men, and there is
Martin delivering the eulogy to a crowd Eddie would have loved,
for they have all turned out for him. Only he isn't here to describe their faces, and their shoes, and their love affairs; he isn't
here to whisper, "Look at that man with the puffed lips, and
those aristocratic hands! He's *drop-dead!*" So's Eddie. And when
we pour outside onto the street afterward, the darkening streets,
the red sky above the rooftops, the sidewalks thronged with
people coming home from work—all seem to demand his presence, or at least his comments on the funeral we have just

attended. The odd thing about a wake is it leaves you feeling very alive afterward. "Who was that *handsome* man with the beard in the third row?" says a friend, supplying words that Eddie would have otherwise; it's the first sign that life goes on. The funeral is reviewed: shoes, beards, friends, strangers. We walk down Second Avenue together in the suits and ties we rarely wear in each other's presence and enter a café. The room is warm, crowded with young men and women who sit in black turtlenecks writing in their journals, like the Hollywood version of an artists' café. We find a table. We notice the man behind the counter making carrot juice has beautiful forearms. A friend tells the story of the oboe player from Minneapolis who came to live with him this summer. Everyone at the table agrees a favorite male model looked wonderful and that Eddie would have loved the crowd who came to his wake. The carrot cake, hot chocolate, and tea arrive, the room gets louder, handsome young men come into the café. Happy to be here, with his three friends, the tourist suddenly takes their four neckties and joins them at their tips over the coffee cups in the center of the table. The tourist doesn't know why he does this; it seems a silly gesture; he suspected the differences in the four neckties might reveal something about each of them, or he wants to unite the quartet at that moment, somehow. When he sees it does not and no one understands what he is doing, he returns them to their shirt fronts and goes on talking about the funeral, watching the people in the room with a wild eagerness, thinking it is still the most extraordinary city, lovely, horrendous, thrilling, sad. And missing one thing, besides sex and drugs: Eddie.

The Fear

THE FEAR IS of course unseemly—as most fear is. People behave at worst with demonic cruelty—at best oddly. Even
among those who are good-hearted, the madness breaks out in
small ways that bring friendships of long standing to an abrupt
end. When the plague began and the television crews of certain
stations refused to work on interviews with people with AIDS, I
wanted to get their names, write them down, publish them on a
list of cowards. When the parents in Queens picketed and refused to send their kids to school; when they kicked Ryan White
out of class in Indiana; when people called in to ask if it was safe
to ride the subway; when Pat Buchanan called for a quarantine of
homosexuals; when they burned down the house in Arcadia,
Florida, I felt a thrilling disgust, an exhilarating contempt, an
anger at the shrill, stupid, mean panic, the alacrity with which
people are converted to lepers and the lepers cast out of the tribe,

the fact that if Fear is contemptible, it is most contemptible in people who have no reason to fear.

Even within the homosexual community, however, there was despicable behavior: men who would not go to restaurants, hospital rooms, wakes, for fear that any contact with other homosexuals might be lethal. At dinner one night in San Francisco in 1982, a friend said, "There's a crack in the glass," after I'd taken a sip of his lover's wine, and took the glass back to the kitchen to replace it—a reaction so swift it took me a moment to realize there was no crack in the glass; the problem was my lips' touching it—homosexual lips, from New York: the kiss of death. I was disgusted then, but the behavior no longer surprises me. AIDS, after all, belongs to the Age of Anxiety. My friend was a germophobe to begin with, who, though homosexual himself, had come to loathe homosexuals. The idea that they could now kill him, or his lover, fit in with his worldview. AIDS fed on his free-floating anxiety about the rest of modern life: the fertilizers, pesticides, toxic waste, additives in food, processing of food, steroids given cattle, salmonella in chickens, killer bees moving up from Brazil, Mexicans sneaking across the border, poisoned water, lead in our pipes, radon in our homes, asbestos in our high schools, mercury in tuna, auto emissions in the air, cigarette smoke in the restaurant, Filipinos on the bus. The society that could make sugar sinister was ready, it would seem, to panic over AIDS, so that when Russia put out the disinformation in its official press that AIDS was the work of a germ-warfare laboratory run by the Pentagon, it was only repeating a charge made by homosexuals convinced that AIDS is a right-wing program to eradicate queers.

God only knows what AIDS will turn out to be, years and years from now. Perhaps, in 2050, *60 Minutes* will reveal it *was* a CIA foul-up. But this general panic, this unease, this sense that the world is out of control and too intimately connected, is not *all* the Fear is among homosexuals. The Fear among homosexuals is personal, physical, and real. It is easy enough to dismiss the idea that the CIA set out to exterminate homosexuals; it is not so easy to dismiss the fact that—having lived in New York during the seventies as a gay man—one can reasonably expect to have been infected. "We've all been exposed," a friend said to me in 1981 on the sidewalk one evening before going off to Switzerland to have his blood recycled—when "exposed" was still the word used to spare the feelings of those who were, someone finally pointed out, "infected." The idea—that everyone had been swimming in the same sea—made little impression on us at first. At first I did not grasp the implications—because then the plague was still so new, and its victims so (relatively) few, that most gay men could still come up with a list of forty to fifty things to distinguish their past, their habits, from those of the men they knew who had it. Five years later, that list is in shreds; one by one, those distinguishing features or habits have been taken away, and the plague reveals itself as something infinitely larger, more various, more random, than was suspected at the start—as common as the flu—indeed, the thing the doctors were predicting a repeat of: the Spanish influenza following World War I.

Predictions like these, above all, intensify the Fear, to the point that one tenses when a story about AIDS comes on the evening news—and wonders: What new sadistic detail? What

new insoluble problem? One looks away when the word is in the
newspaper headline and turns to the comics instead. One hopes
the phone will not ring with news of yet another friend diagnosed, because one can always trace a flare-up of the Fear—an
AIDS anxiety attack: that period when you are certain you have
It, and begin making plans for your demise—to some piece of
news, or several, that came through the television or the telephone. Sometimes they are so numerous, and simultaneous, that
you are undone—like the man walking down the boardwalk on
Fire Island with a friend one evening on their way to dance, who,
after a quiet conversation at dinner, suddenly threw himself
down on the ground and began screaming, "We're all going to
die, we're all going to die!" He did. Sometimes it hits like that. It
appears in the midst of the most ordinary circumstances—like
the man on that same beach, who, in the middle of a cloudless summer afternoon, turned to my friend and said, "What is the point of
going on?" ("To bear witness," my friend responded.) The Fear is
there all the time, but it comes in surges, like electricity—
activated, triggered, almost always, by specific bad news.

The media are full of bad news, of course—the stories of
breakthroughs, of discoveries, of new drugs, seem to have sub-
sided now into a sea of disappointment. They do not sound the
note of relief and hope and exultation they once did—that dream
that one evening you would be brushing your teeth, and your
roommate, watching the news in the living room, would shout,
"It's over!" and you would run down the hall and hear the
Armistice declared. Instead, the media carry the pronouncements

of the Harvard School of Public Health, the World Health Organization, dire beyond our wildest nightmares: What began as a strange disease ten or twelve homosexuals in New York had contracted becomes the Black Death. Journalists, as Schopenhauer said, are professional alarmists, and have only fulfilled their usual role: scaring their readers. They are scaring them not just to sell newspapers, however, or to keep them in their seats till the next commercial. They are scaring them so that they will protect themselves, and, at the same time, inducing despair in those already infected. There's the dilemma: They're all watching the same TV, reading the same newspapers.

After a while, the Fear is so ugly you feel like someone at a dinner party whose fellow guests are being taken outside and shot as you concentrate politely on your salad. There is the school of thought that says the Fear is a form of stress, and stress enhances the virus. Like the man so afraid of muggers he somehow draws them to him, the Fear is said to make itself come true, by those who believe in mind control. As a friend of mine (so fearful of the disease he refused to have sex for four years) said, "I got everything I resisted." So one becomes fearful even of the Fear. The Fear can be so wearing, so depressing, so constant that a friend who learned he had AIDS said, on hearing the diagnosis, "Well, it's a lot better than worrying about it."

He also said, "I wasn't doing anything anyone else wasn't." Which explains the Fear more succinctly than anything else: Tens of thousands were doing the same thing in the seventies. Why, then, should some get sick and not others? Isn't it logical to expect everyone will, eventually? The Fear is so strong it causes people to change cities, to rewrite their pasts in order to imagine they were doing less than everyone else; because the most unnerving thing about the plague is its location in the Past, the Time allotted to it.

Were AIDS a disease which, once contracted, brought death within forty-eight hours of exposure, it would be a far more easily avoided illness—but because it is not, because it is invisible, unknown, for such a long period of time, because it is something people got before they even knew it existed (with each passing year, the time lag gets longer), the Fear of AIDS is limitless. Who has not had sex within the last seven years—once? (The nun in San Francisco who got AIDS from a blood transfusion given her during an operation to set her broken leg, and died, her superiors said, without anger or bitterness.) (The babies who get it in the womb.) There's a memory—of an evening, an incident—to justify every fear. And nothing exists that will guarantee the fearful that even if they are functioning now they will not get caught in the future. The phrase that keeps running through the fearful mind is: Everyone was healthy before he got sick. One has to have two programs, two sets of responses, ready at all times: (a) Life, (b) Death. The switch from one category to the other can come at any moment, in the most casual way. At the dentist's, or putting on your sock. Did that shin bruise a little too easily? Is that a new mole? Is the sinus condition that won't go away just a sinus condition? Do you feel a bit woozy standing at the kitchen sink? Do you want to lie down? Is the Fear making you woozy or the virus? Have you had too many colds this past spring to be just colds? Thus the hyperconsciousness of the body begins.

Your body—which you have tended, been proud of—is something you begin to view with suspicion, mistrust. Your body is someone you came to a party with but you'd like to ditch, only you promised to drive him home. Your body is a house with a thief inside who wants to rob you of everything in it. Your body could be harboring It, even as you go about your business. This keeps you on edge. You stop, for instance, looking in mirrors—or at your body in the shower—because the skin, all of a sudden, seems as vast as Russia: a huge terrain, a monumental wall, on which tiny handwriting may suddenly appear. The gums, the tongue, the face, the foot, the forearm, the leg: billions of cells waiting to go wrong. Because you read that sunburn depresses the immune system, you no longer go out in the sun. You stay in the house—as if already an invalid; you cancel all thoughts of traveling in airplanes because you heard flights can trigger the pneumonia and because you want to be home when it happens, not in some hotel room in Japan or San Diego.

And so the Fear constricts Life. It suffocates, till one evening its prey snaps—gets in the car and drives to the rest stop, or bar, or baths, to meet another human being; and has sex. Sometimes has sex—sometimes just talks about the Fear, because a conversation about the danger of sex sometimes replaces sex itself. The Fear is a god to which offerings must be made before sex can commence. Sometimes it refuses the offering. If it does not, it takes its share of the harvest afterward. Sex serves the Fear more slavishly than anything. Even safe sex leads to the question: Why was I even doing something that *required* condoms? The aftermath of sex is fear *and* loathing. Death is a hunk. Sex and terror are twins. AIDS is a national program of aversion therapy.

The Fear is also extremely self-centered, above all personal, and leads you to acts of insensitivity. One day you spill your fear about the sex you just had to a friend who—you remember too late—has had AIDS for a couple of years now. He has lived with his own fear for two years. Your friend merely listens calmly, says what you did does not seem unsafe, and then remarks, "What I'm getting from what you've been saying is that you're still afraid." Of course, you want to reply, of *course* I'm still afraid!

"But you have no reason to be," he says, from the height, the eminence, of his own fear, digested, lived with, incorporated into his own life by now. "If you don't have it now, you won't."

Another friend has told you, "The doctors think we're about to see a second wave of cases, the ones who contracted it in 1981." Going home on the subway, your fear takes the form of superstition: He should never have said that! He himself had said (a remark you've never forgotten) that he was diagnosed just at the point when—after three years of abstinence—he thought he had escaped. It's the time lag, of course, the petri dish in which the Fear thrives. Of course, you are afraid; every male homosexual who lived in New York during the seventies is scared shitless. And a bit unstable, withdrawn, and crazy.

The tactlessness of venting your fear to a friend who already has been diagnosed is symptomatic of the Fear. People who are afraid are seldom as considerate as those who are not. The ironic

thing about my last visit to New York was that the pair of lovers I
know who have AIDS were cheerful, calm, gracious, well-behaved.
Those who did not were nervous wrecks: depressed, irritable, isolated, withdrawn, unwilling to go out at night, in bed by ten, under a blanket, with anxiety and a VCR. The Fear is not fun to live
with, though when shared, it can produce occasional, hysterical
laughter. The laughter vanishes, however, the moment you leave
the apartment building and find yourself alone on the street—
falls right off your face as you slip instantly back into the mood
you were in before you went to visit your friend. The Fear breeds
depression. The depression breeds anger (which must pale beside
the anger of people who have it toward those who don't: Why
me? Why should *he* escape?). Friendships come to an end over incidents that would have been jokes before. People withdraw from
each other so they don't have to go through the suffering of each
other's illness. People behave illogically. One night a friend refuses to eat from a buffet commemorating a dead dancer because
so many of the other guests have AIDS—"They shouldn't have
served finger food," he mutters—but he leaves the wake with a
young handsome Brazilian who presumably doesn't, goes home,
and has sex. We all have an explanation for such actions, for our
choices of what we will do and what we won't; we all have a ratio-
nale for our superstitions. Most of it *is* superstition, because that
is what the Fear produces and always has. Some of it is just mud-
dled thinking, like the logic of the nightclub patrons in Miami
who said they did not worry about getting AIDS there because it
cost ten dollars to get in. And some of it is perfectly rational, like
the apprehension that convinces people they should not take the

Test because they would rather not live with the knowledge that they have antibodies to the virus. (Today, the news announces a home test that will tell you in three minutes if you do, or don't— not much time for counseling!)

The Test is the most concentrated form of the Fear there is— which is why people tell you not to take it if you think you will have trouble handling the results. Why should we know? The fact is things are happening in our bodies, our blood, all the time we know nothing of; the hole in the dike of our immune systems may appear at any moment, and is always invisible, silent, unadvertised.

When does a person begin to develop cancer? When does a tumor start to grow? When does the wall of the heart begin to weaken? Do you want to know? With AIDS, there is presumably something in hiding, in the brain, the tissues, waiting for some moment to begin its incredibly fast and protean reproduction. It may be waiting—or reproducing—as I type this. This is the Fear that is utterly personal—that makes you think imagining is worse than reality. This is what makes you think: I must know, I can't bear this, I'll take the Test. So you drive over one hot afternoon to do it, thinking of the letter from a woman whose nephew just died at home of AIDS: "Tony even tested Negative two months before he died." What fun. You feel as if you are driving not toward the county health department but the Day of Judgment. In my right hand, I give you Life, in my left, Death. What will you do, the voice asks, when you find out? How will you live? How do people with AIDS drive the car, fall asleep at night, face the neighbors, deal with solitude? The stupendous cruelty of this disease crashes in upon you. And so you bargain with God. You apologize, and make vows. You ask: How could this have happened? How could I have reached this point? Where did I make the turn that got me on *this* road? Every test you have ever taken, written or oral—the book reports; the thesis examination; the spelling bees; those afternoons walking home from school as far as you could before turning the page of your test to see the grade on a corner where no one could see your reaction; the day you got drafted; the day you found out whether you were going to Vietnam—all pale, or come back, in one single concentrated tsunami of terror at this moment.

In eighteenth-century Connecticut, Jonathan Edwards preached a sermon called "Sinners in the Hands of an Angry God," which was so terrifying that women in the congregation fainted. Imagine you are a spider, he said, suspended on a web over the fire—the fire of Hell—by the grace of God. Some things never change. The Fear, like the sermon, feeds on the imagination. But whenever you're with someone who faces this disease daily with composure, calm, humor, and his or her own personality intact, you realize how deforming, how demeaning, how subject to the worst instincts it is.

Tragic Drag

ONE NIGHT IN 1970, I think, friends took me to a very small theater on Tenth or Eleventh Street to see a play called *Hot Ice*. It was a play about cryogenics, and it cost five dollars, I believe; no one explained what we were about to see, yet everyone I went with—people who had seen *Turds in Hell* or *Bluebeard*—had about him a certain air that implied there was no need to explain, I would soon see why one went to any play Charles Ludlam and the Ridiculous Theatrical Company put on.

At the time, I'd stopped going to the theater—mainly because the baths were far more thrilling, more dramatic, and cheaper than anything on Broadway—and because I basically agree with a friend of mine who said theaters should be shut down for ten years and be allowed to open after a decade's darkness if, and only if, there was some justification for it. (And who got up during the second act of a play once and said—when I hissed, "Where are you going?"—"Home, to watch *Masterpiece Theater*.") That was the problem. Sitting in a theater uptown, one was always won-dering: *Why did they have everyone drive in from the suburbs, get a babysitter, come uptown on the subway, for this? Why couldn't we be at home in our underwear, watching this on TV?* With Charles Ludlam one never asked these questions. Uptown, one found oneself observing people in their living rooms—or, as the "legiti-mate" theater continued to shrink from a news-clogged world it could not compete with, their dining rooms (*Table Manners, The Dining Room*), as if the family melodrama would someday be dis-tilled down to single pieces of furniture (*The Bidet*). On the local five o'clock news you watched, as you dressed for the theater, a man walking a wire strung between the twin towers of the World Trade Center; when you got to the theater, you saw a woman cleaning her house before she committed suicide. That strange custom of applauding the set when the curtain went up (so often on a plush Manhattan apartment, reproduced to the last book on the library shelf) seemed as artificial as the plays on Broadway at the time; we might as well have been clapping for the designer rooms at Kips Bay, or the windows at Altman's. At *Hot Ice* there was no curtain, if I recall; the stage, very small, depicted the labo-ratory of a mad scientist (the character that lay beneath, behind, within, it seemed, almost all the roles Charles Ludlam took on), and from the moment he came onstage, I knew something was going to happen.

Nothing is so ephemeral as a theatrical performance—it even differs from night to night—and, in an age when songs, concerts, films, books, the explosion of the *Challenger*, the inauguration of a president, can be reproduced over and over again, hoarded and stored, what Ludlam did on his little stage is remembered solely by people who happened to see him. Writing about him now seems dumb, like analyzing laughter, which no doubt Ludlam did, but never in front of us, onstage; in front of us, onstage, he simply induced it. He induced more than that, however; in any performance of *Camille*, half the people in the audience were tearing up and half were shrieking with laughter—at the same line. That was Charles Ludlam. In a country whose critics, and actors, are always bemoaning the absence of a repertory company, Charles Ludlam, and the Ridiculous Theatrical Company he founded, were just that: a place we could go year after year, to new play after new play, to be entertained. How he did it I don't know. Proust had trouble analyzing Sarah Bernhardt as Berma in *Remembrance of Things Past*—and Ludlam was, like Bernhardt, just an actor. And playwright. And director. And designer. And—it would sound ridiculous, I suppose, if I said genius, but that was how I felt that night in 1970, sitting on the edge of my seat at *Hot Ice,* open-mouthed as any child at a Punch-and-Judy show.

Charles Ludlam *did* a Punch-and-Judy show, in which he took all twenty-two parts, and that was only one aspect of his theater mania: Nothing in the performing arts was foreign to him, or unused. Puppets, wigs, ball gowns, snoods, musclemen, fake fog, mechanical fish, daggers, goblets, vacuum chambers, flowers, and real flush toilets found places in his theater. His theater was *very*—theatrical. If someone had never seen a play in his life, he could have gone to Charles Ludlam and seen virtually all of theater encapsulated in one performance. Ludlam was comprehensive—pure theater. Which we were starved for—

driven to his little group by the staleness of Broadway, the fatu-
ities of a mass-produced, television-dominated, film-and-book-
soaked century that gave equal time to the fall of Beirut and
the fire in Michael Jackson's hair started by a commercial for
Pepsi Cola. Drowning in what Godard said the West had simply too much of—Culture; on the lam from history, novels,
films, the *New York Review of Books*—and none of them any
FUN! Grenades ready to explode in our seats when Ludlam
came onstage—pins pulled by this short, bald man with a big
nose, large dark eyes, and a little mouth. There was something
about Ludlam—no matter what the costume, wig, or role, he
held you in thrall. There was an insane, cracked quality in this
smoldering anarchist of kitsch that made him, no matter what
the scene or part, the center of attention. Onstage he had the air
of a madman, really, listening to some lurid music of the spheres
the rest of the cast could not hear. This performer, who looked,
on the street, like the superintendent of an apartment building on
Jane Street, or a janitor sweeping up at a high school on the
Lower East Side, or a salesman who sold trusses out of an office
in midtown Manhattan, was, when he came onstage, an actor so
charismatic, so in possession of his method, that no matter how
bad the play—and there were a few one did not *rush* to recom-
mend to friends—or how mundane the particular passage, one
never took one's eyes off him. Ludlam—and his *gothic* eyes—
always seemed at the least perturbed; at most, as loony as
Rasputin.

The greatest comedy has this element of madness, I think—
the sense that we've shoved off, there are no limits, the actor is

wacko. (Mel Brooks, not Woody Allen; Richard Pryor, not Bill Cosby.) Lunacy and cunning pulled Ludlam's chariot with competing force. The saying "Life is a tragedy to those who feel, a comedy to those who think," is too schematic, after all. Because most of us think *and* feel, if not always simultaneously, the pressure of the two creates an urge in some of us to just—*lose it* now and then. That's what the cult of Dionysus was all about, and the cult of Dionysus is where Theater started. You could lose it with Charles Ludlam. It would be pointless to subject Ludlam to a dissertation—he was too funny—and yet no one was more grounded in theater's ancient roots than he; like a child running through the contents of his bedroom closet, putting on fake noses, mustaches, pulling out toy airplanes, little plastic gladiators, goldfish bowls, ray-guns, Cleopatra wigs, he always gave the impression of having assembled the particular play from a magic storeroom in which he kept, like some obsessed bag lady, every prop and character that two thousand years of Western history had washed up on the shores of a childhood on Long Island. If uptown you watched depressed people in their living rooms, when you went to the little theater that became Ludlam's permanent home, you sat down before a palace in Carthage, a temple, a crypt, a tomb, a railroad station, a yacht cruising the Aegean with billionaire and diva taking the sun—everything *but* the living room. Instead of a *hausfrau* committing suicide, Camille in Paris, gayer times, other centuries, cultures, codes of conduct: the gamut of Western culture's books, plots, and characters. Ludlam added subjects, when the theater was subtracting them; introduced new plays, when the houses uptown were dark for lack of original work; became more theatrical, when most of the lore and craft of theater seemed to have slipped away to Hollywood.

Ludlam did make movies—even appeared in a television sit-com I tuned to once by accident—but his genius belonged to the theater. Theater was his *subject*. He mined past plays for his exaggerations, intonations, looks, monologues, asides, settings, props. He made fun of all its pretense. Once Ludlam sat down on a toilet onstage in *Stage Blood*, delivered Hamlet's soliloquy, stood up, pulled the chain, and in that single flush sent up every apartment erected on a Broadway stage. In Ludlam, realism was make-believe; make-believe was the joke (and the delight)—so that we gasped when, as a Carthaginian princess about to be purified before her marriage in *Salammbo*, he raised his skirt to reveal what looked like a vagina for ritual shaving. And we thrilled when the cardboard train came sliding onstage to deliver Galas (the diva whose first line, at the station café, was, "I'll have the veal cutlet"). The make-believe train was the sort of thing children would be delighted by, but then that is what we all were, at a Ludlam play: children. Smart, jaded, ironic, sophisticated children, watching a magician dress up, caress, and bring to life again a theater whose corpse the "legitimate" theater was too sophisticated, too tasteful, too realistic, too something to rouse.

It seems that simple: Ludlam *used* theater—its most ancient, vulgar tricks—when no one else was able to. He did so, chiefly, by making fun of it. That was all he needed to give us entrance to realms one could no longer visit any other way. The god of originality in the arts, after all, is mean: One can no longer offer up on his altar a sonata like Schubert's, a poem like Keats's. One can only write *The Importance of Being Earnest* or paint the *Mona Lisa* once. (So today we get electronic music, and Julian Schnabel.) Ludlam found a way around the altar—had a key that unlocked the door of that chamber behind the deity in which all those heroes and heroines, villains and viragos (Camille, Bluebeard, Hamlet, Wagner, Callas—and Houdini), were waiting to amuse us again. The key, the rejuvenating alchemy, was satire. Farce. A unique aesthetic in which the classic became avant-garde. Who else but Ludlam would have staged an obscure novel by Flaubert as a send-up of Hollywood epics about gladiators with the sort of chests that made Groucho Marx say he never went to films in which the men's tits were bigger than the women's? (Ludlam merely hired a group of muscle builders from a local gym.) Who else but Ludlam would have given us *Camille?* With such conviction—such art—that half the audience was laughing while the other half groaned, and what the audience was doing changed from moment to moment, line to line, syllable to syllable, as we followed the rises and dips of that incredible voice—that resonant, dark, wounded, demonic, sinuous, whimsical, whining, wheedling, imperious instrument?

Ludlam was also a master of the punch line—the mainstay of Woody Allen—which punctured the balloon of High Art but fast. (When Camille is dying, her lover Armand ends a florid declaration of his love with the words, "Toodle-oo, Marguerite!" When Galas lists the reasons she wants to die, the last one is, "And there's nothing on television tonight!") But the punch lines came only after we'd drunk rapturously of the Real Thing. One may ask, "What did we know of the Real Thing?" "Tragedy is dead," said the critic. We could no longer stage this seriously. Our teeth were fluoridated, our theater air-conditioned. Too modern, too rational, too prosperous, too aware of genocide to care about individual fate. Why, then, did we sit rapt before dying Camille? Ludlam was our only showcase of the bravura roles, the classic acting of a sort one could no longer find, in the Age of Realism—in a culture whose solution for grief is grief counseling, whose reaction to catastrophe is stress management and acupuncture, Ludlam played Tragedy. He played both Tragedy and Farce and refused to tell us which was which. He died onstage of tuberculosis, or heartache, and left us not knowing whether to laugh or cry, suspended somewhere (with parted lips) between the two; so that when he raised his gloved hand to his lips, as Camille, and coughed those three little coughs—just three—the audience both howled and stopped laughing altogether.

He also performed at a time when what was underground and what was homosexual were one—there was a whole decade, after all, between Candy Darling and Harvey Fierstein—and his two greatest roles were basically Tragic Drag: women whom fortune dumps in a rather rude way—Camille (whom Ludlam played more than once, a favorite he could always resurrect) and Galas. It seems now in retrospect that all art presupposes a certain health, leisure, freedom in which to laugh at things that in life are actually horrid and brutal. We all could scream at the three little coughs that caused earlier generations to sob—or Galas's lament, "Everyone I know is either dead or in Monte Carlo!"—because at the time we were worried primarily about our *latissimus dorsi*. Ludlam was described to me, in fact, that night I saw *Hot Ice,* as

an ornament of gay New York—like the Loft, the Everard—
pleasures of a segment of society that in 1970 was Fun. In the
theater that night were people who had come to the city, to work
and play, for whom Ludlam was the adored genius whose next
play (no tortured intellectual he, observing long periods of silence before he had something new to say; Ludlam put on plays
the way bakers bake bread) was a piece of news joyously transmit-
ted in the hallways of the baths. When Ludlam turned, in
Camille, to his maid in a boudoir in Paris and said (in that rumi-
nating, pathetic tone), "Throw another faggot on the fire!," the
maid respectfully replied, "There are no faggots in the house,
Madame." And Ludlam, rising on one arm on the chaise longue
to look directly out at his audience with that morose expression
would say, "What? No *faggots* in the house?," whereupon whole
ages of repression went up in shrieks.

There were lots of faggots in the house, of course—bronzed,
muscular habitués of gyms and Fire Island, in plaid shirts, muscles, and mustaches—and if everything Ludlam did was ironic, a
double entendre of sorts, so were their lives, and Camille and
Galas spoke to that. Ludlam was superb in a lot of other roles (*Le
Bourgeois Avant-Garde, Salammbo, The Mystery of Irma Vep*), but
there were plays I let run without making the effort to see, because they were, as a friend fumed one time when I asked how
the new one was, "hardly high school." (Some high school! What
Bluebeard said might apply as a small understatement to Ludlam's work: "When I'm good I'm very good, and when I'm bad,
I'm . . . not bad.") *Camille* and *Galas,* however, were of another
order. Drag is a profound joke—the fundamental homosexual

joke, no doubt: The Woman at Bay, wounded but triumphant, lascivious or frigid, repressed or mad, rings all the notes, high and low. That which appalls the race in real life (change of sex roles) onstage unchains. Charles Ludlam was the greatest drag I've ever seen. It ceased to be drag, in fact, or acting: It was art. That mouth, those eyes—that voice, that fan! That insidious send-up of absolutely everything! That superb evocation of the classic, the romantic, the aristocratic. (Yes, aristocratic. The secret wish of every homosexual—the drag queen as Queen. Of the *Universe*.) We sat in our jeans and T-shirts in a city, culture, and century flooded with fake emotion and took *Camille* utterly seriously— the only way we *could* take it: as a joke.

Alas, the veneer of culture is quite thin, and make-believe no match for reality. The misery of nineteenth-century tuberculars is no longer a subject for exquisite farce; and this generation—for whom tragedy could be performed only *as* farce—is now having to separate them again, and put farce in the attic. Not only is Charles Ludlam gone, it seems, so is humor. One no longer can make jokes about death. One can no longer make jokes at all— the curtain's down. Talleyrand is supposed to have said that those who never lived before the Revolution never knew *douceur de vie*—well, those who never saw Charles Ludlam before the plague missed some brilliant moments in the theater. Oh, were they brilliant. Oh, was he funny. Oh, is he dead. Oh, is this plague—ridiculous.

Beauty NOW

BEAUTY NOW. HAIR, Eyes, Lips, Makeup, Fashion NOW. NEW ICONS. What Everyone's Talking About: Books, Plays, Music, Food, Travel, Eskimos, Chess, Virgins.

"SOMETIMES IN LIFE," someone marvelously French said (oh, all right! *Proust*), "all we need is a change of weather." Well darling, it's PUMPKIN-Time in the Big MANGO. *Mejor dicho:* Autumn in New York. Why does it set the heart *dancing?* Because we're back in town after a long, slow, DEFENSIVE vacation at the beach and WE FEEL GOOD ABOUT OURSELVES. (Not to mention how good we LOOK.) Time to take stock. To choose what in the new fall season is right FOR US. To strengthen Beauty Points: Attitude, Hair, Eyes, Lips, Skin, Makeup, Knees, Body. Time for buckling down with all that is best in WHAT'S NEW: A NEW diet, a NEW kind of Romance, a NEW You. What's NEW in what WE SEE for YOU this FALL '85—the BEST fall of your lives—begins with:

Beauty NOW. A NEW APPROACH. Those long, pensive walks you took on Fire Island, Laguna Beach, or Cape Cod in late August have PAID OFF. Those lonely nights midweek when your house was empty, and instead of doing something risky like visiting the RACK you lay on the deck listening to a Vivaldi guitar concerto, wondering "What's a flower for?," are yielding BIG DIVIDENDS: People see you're at your PEAK OF BEAUTY. Of course, you *used* to stop and chat with these adoring FANS, but this fall you have a reserved and distant and MYSTERIOUS air. People wonder WHY you're not cruising them. Why you don't LOCK EYES ON THE STREET. *You* know the reason. It's simple. YOU'RE SCARED. At your job—which will be, this fall, MUCH more absorbing, fulfilling, and interesting than it has EVER been before (and you know why), you keep that GUARDED yet OPEN feeling as you mix with all the DIVINE FLESH that congregates in our city.

IMAGE. A cold and silver SEA seen from the stone cell of an IRISH MONK in the fourteenth century, transcribing a text of Aristotle in the most BEAUTIFUL CALLIGRAPHY the world has ever known. YOU: a secret, wild rose growing on a misty, cool, high promontory outside his window—even though you're in the middle of perhaps the most HYSTERICAL city in the world, or even (who knows) some little speed trap down SOUTH (which has its OWN hysteria). Beauty NOW is CALM. Beauty NOW is HEALTH. The NEW ICONS are: Virgins, Stone Age Tribes, ESKIMOS, Sophomores in Town on a Class Trip, Anybody from North Dakota, Chinese chess champions with BRACES. The OLD ICONS—hot men, used men,

Italian baggage handlers, Puerto Rican messengers. Syrian taxi drivers, dark, mustached men in their prime—are OUT OUT OUT. *Don't touch!* Glance at them MAYBE on the windows of airline offices as you walk by on this CRISP, FALL AFTERNOON, *not* directly. (They won't look back anyway, since everyone is practicing the NEW RESERVE.) BONUS: Glancing at the plate glass window of the AVIANCA office lets you see your—

Hair NOW. Hair NOW is of course short on the sides, thick on top, though you could break away from the pack by growing an AFRO. (*Live.*) Hair NOW, in whatever style *you* choose to present it, is, of course, HEALTH-HAIR. Remember your FOCUS in fall '85: Carrots, raw greens, and other vitamin-A-rich foods FEED Follicles. DANGER: If some evening your haircut is INCREDIBLE—SO GOOD you must go out, then do it, but simply to SHOW YOUR HAIRCUT. The theme for fall '85? *Look But Do Not Touch.* (Remember Mom when her hair and nails were *Just Right* before going out?) Try taking your FABULOUS HAIRCUT to SAFE locations like: the Guggenheim, Saint Patrick's, your favorite J.O. Club. (And *remember,* at the latter, there is no outfit on earth more DEVASTATING than simple white Jockey shorts and T-shirt. DESIGNER LABELS: *VERBOTEN.*) Or take your haircut out for a WALK. Wherever you are, remember: Hair NOW is about being STRESS-FREE, and INNER PEACE comes from knowing you are ALIVE and committed to REMAINING SO in the near term. Health-Hair NOW is the expression of that commitment, and so, darling are—

Lips NOW. Lips *used* to be for: Sucking, Licking, Hissing, Talking Dirty, Slurping. Now they're for: Discussing the Meaning of Existence, Prayer, and Song. Lips NOW have never looked more FABULOUS because they are PRISTINE. Join the *Gay Men's Chorus!* Gargle regularly with warm water, baking soda, and/or salt, to keep the edges and inner lining of the mouth MOIST and RED. Don't GNAW at your lower lip even though the New Reserve may induce TENSION. Remember your FOCUS: Lips are COMPOSED, SERENE, yet GENEROUS. Lips '85 convey a WEALTH OF EXPERIENCE, *and* a wealth of WISDOM. Lips '85 send a message: NO. *We are no longer doing certain things.* This can be HARD ON LIPS. LIPS '85 are used to saying, "I DON'T DO THAT NOW." Because SOMEONE PISSED IN THE POOL, darling! Because we all realize now that anonymous (Let-Yourself-GO) sex is OUT, unless you want to spend this FALL '85 petrified over every pimple and cold sore and ache. Lips '85 want to know: What about Safe SEX? SAFE SEX can be FABOU for the lips—if they don't have to EXPLAIN IT to the person first. Whose lips enjoy NEGOTIATING rules of lovemaking before sex? KEY: Look for people ON YOUR LEVEL: AWARE, WITH IT, KNOWING, ON THE CREST OF THE WAVE. If you should see a HUMPY ANGEL you *cannot* pass up, use your LIPS '85 to find OUT what he knows. And if he doesn't know ENOUGH (and LIPS '85 are all about KNOWING. Why else do you live in the most fabulous city in the world?), then simply give him the telephone number of a FRIEND who will explain on your behalf Condoms, Hydrogen Peroxide, Clorox, Oxynol-9 (and let's not kid ourselves any longer about Kissing: I know this is tough on die-hard romantics, but grow up). Sally Slut says to herself, "If I have to go over there and raise the issue of DEATH with that gorgeous man, I'd rather not bother." (Makes sense, Sally.) *Sally Sensible makes the effort.* Both ask, "What IS sex, anyway?" or (more accurately) "What WAS sex?"—before going ahead with it. Use Lips to redefine, RETHINK what same-sex desire is *really* all about. Use Lips to sing fabulous, sophisticated, bluesy RODGERS & HART ballads that still express JUST HOW WE FEEL. CONSIDER: Taking your FABULOUS NEW LIPS to church. Lips '85 look great in a PEW because PRAYING and FOLLOWING THE LITURGY are SAFE SEX. BONUS: At the coffee hours after the service at Dignity or the gay synagogue, you may meet men who are there for something other than INSTANT oral gratification. Use your Lips to discuss THE SOUL. (You HAVE one, darling. You just MISPLACED it during the seventies! It's someplace around the apartment. LOOK FOR IT.) And while you do, practice FACIAL ISOMETRICS. Because Lips '85 are both PHYSICAL and SPIRITUAL Lips, CENTERED, CALM, COMPOSED Lips, and so, darling, are—

Eyes NOW. Eyes this fall are VERY IMPORTANT, more important than ever before, more important than LIPS, because they are—quite frankly—our CHIEF SEXUAL ORGAN this season. BE CREATIVE. Take mental photographs of HOT, HUMPY MEN all over town to be developed later in the silence of your own bedroom where you will be having SAFE SEX with yourself. (The body simply does not like foreign sperm.) The hot, humpy PUERTO RICAN MESSENGER hanging on to the subway strap next to yours? DEVOUR HIM WITH YOUR EYES. FOCUS on a LIMB, a BUTTOCK, the shadow of a beard on his square jaw, a muscle flickering beneath the skin. (HOT STUFF, darling.) You CAN have sex with *les yeux*. (See Wordsworth, "The Daffodils." Or Cavafy, the DIVINE Alexandrian poet who had sex simply by EXAMINING fabrics with a cute salesman behind the counter. BE CREATIVE.) Whether you RUN, or do TAI CHI, or SWIM, take in the sight of SWEATY ATHLETES in their UNSPEAKABLE BEAUTY— the stain that a perspiring ass makes on PALE GRAY SWEAT-PANTS, the way HAIR clings to the forehead of someone who has spent SIX HOURS playing BASKETBALL—as you USE SPORTS to SMOOTH YOURSELF OUT during this period when oral satisfaction is being denied. *(Type A personalities especially:* Take thirty-minute SWIMS three times a week. Use goggles to protect your eyes. Do not take too long in the shower. Be careful not to *slip* in the shower, because the floors of many gym shower rooms these days are *covered* with spermatozoa.) SUGGESTION: Get into the pool in the lane next to someone CUTE. Make your FLIP-TURN when HE does, so you end up *face-to-crotch* with his *Speedo* underwater! OR: Swim the CRAWL slightly *behind* him, so you can see his ass tighten and relax with his flutter kick, and the flare of his back, and those beautiful chests coming toward you in the other lanes. Because—

EYES '85 are all about PERIPHERAL VISION. They are HONEST, FORTHRIGHT, WARM, but CLOSED.

Consider going to the GYM at odd hours, if the visual stimuli of rush hour overload the circuits. Go LATE when the gym is nearly EMPTY and you do not have to worry about being caught STARING directly at other weight lifters, or TRIPPING on the track as you run looking down at the SEXPOT punching the bag beneath you on the gym floor. CHANGE gyms if yours produces an urge to visit the Baths. Visit the BATHS if VERY FIRM about Safe Sex (this is only for advanced students) for visual feasts of gorgeous homosexuals DENYING DEATH. Less Advanced: Take architectural walking tours of the city—at odd hours; avoid cruisy parks. HOP A TRAIN Up the Hudson to see AUTUMN. (Now that you are still alive, life has never seemed so *precious* to you, and all its extraordinary beauty.) Use the energy left over from NOT HAVING SEX to EXERCISE your eyes by: Paying bills on time, *devouring* the letters of Proust, Henry, William, Alice James, Thomas Mann, Bernard Shaw, Bismarck, Goethe. Finish Robert Musil's *The Man Without Qualities.* WRITE a five-act opera based on same. Watch the man in the building behind yours undress at night. Get to know the PORN you stored years ago under the bed. EXPAND your CONCEPT OF PORN by finding nearly everything you see EROTIC. (The New Celibates know all about this FABULOUS BONUS.) Jerk off with a small mirror on the shelf opposite the toilet seat to show JUST YOUR HAND on your genitals. AVOID PIG EYES on the street. Remember—if America were an Islamic Republic (and more and more people are thinking it SHOULD BE), you might be wearing CHADORS, leaving ONLY the eyes (barely) exposed, which is what EYES '85 are ALL ABOUT. OR: Use your FABULOUS, EDUCATED EYES to make your apartment PRISSY—use enough period furniture, porcelain, ormolu to make a penis

THINK TWICE before getting hard; *or* create a space TOO EMBARRASSING to ask another human being back to: Village NIGHTMARE! *Or:* If TERRIBLY SECURE in the New Restraint, make your room IRRESISTIBLE for those evenings you'll be asking friends over to discuss History: *Sex in the Seventies,* or the latest kiss-and-tell biography of Tennessee Williams, because NOW THAT NO ONE IS MAKING LOVE TO YOU, you need the emotional BONDS *friends* provide more than ever, *and* books about Other People's Sex Lives. When you MUST GET OUT, go to the Eagle and LOOK at other men. (Remembering the rule this season is: *Mira Pero No Toques.*) (Has anything at the Eagle REALLY changed?) WATCH the new plays, films, cabaret that always EXPLODE between now and the holidays. CHOOSE the J.O. Club that is right for YOU. Is DANCING your perfect Sex Substitute? Then OGLE the HOT, HANDSOME, PUMPED-UP GYM BODIES, PERFECT DELTOIDS in a sweaty discotheque. If this leads to the balcony, STAY HOME. (*There are people fresh out of the hospital up there.*) SUGGESTION: Spend Saturday NIGHT parked in front of your TV. Look for: Diet Soda commercials—*pornographic!*—or the obligatory scene by the pool in *Love Boat,* with humpy L.A. extras parading in the background. (*Danger:* Don't watch the scene the Main Actors are playing—this may bring your T-cell count DOWN.) Try reading CYNTHIA OZICK. Or—better yet—use the mirror in your bathroom to perfect your—

Makeup NOW. *Incredible. Revolutionary. Unheard of.* Industry types will tell you this year's eyeliner and blush are based on smoky, woodsy, fall colors, but we are under too much pressure, personally and historically, to put out that line of shit. Smoky, woodsy colors, darling, are NOT In. Nor are pastels, peaches, or the injection of *sheep placenta from Bulgaria*. BE HONEST. In the old days weren't we the first to shatter *oppressive Makeup Myth* by telling you, quite simply, there is no chemical in all of Estée Lauder, Max Factor, OR Clinique's bottomless vats to compare with the GLOW a really marvelous, time-consuming, no-holds-barred, midafternoon *you-know-what* could give you (and WASN'T IT, once-in-a-lifetime, the TRUTH?). *That's all over now!* Makeup '85 is the VERY LITTLE SEX glow. The SAFE SEX, or NO SEX, glow is slightly different—it can even look a bit DEAD—but not to worry. With all the chlorine from the pool you'll be doing thirty miles of LAPS in this fall each month to CALM DOWN, you will look POSITIVELY ETHEREAL. Be DECISIVE. DUMP the Queen Helene Face Mask, the cucumber facial, the superfatted soap in the TRASH. WE ARE TALKING CLEAR, UNOBSTRUCTED YOU. We are talking the ALMOST NO SEX glow. Makeup NOW is totally REALISTIC. HONEST. SENSIBLE. Discipline is STRICT, faces are held ABOVE the steaming collard greens while your pores say: *Bonjour,* vitamin A! Put your *punim* RIGHT INTO the bouillabaisse, no matter how fashionable the restaurant! Bee Pollen? MAINLINE IT! SUGGESTION: Put a little sign above the bathroom mirror that says: 1. I will wash my face every night. 2. I will not let anyone sit on it. The first involves: Distilled water, a Neutral Soap, at least TWENTY RINSES before patting dry with a CLEAN TOWEL. The second involves GOING STRAIGHT TO BED, where you will be getting lots of GOOD,

SOLID SLEEP this Fall because SUPERB SLEEP is ESSEN-
TIAL to your—

Body NOW. Demands getting to KNOW YOUR BODY.
And who knows it better than you? *For starters:* KNEES are in
wonderful shape, because you're not ON THEM anymore, and
you're careful when you RUN to do it on indoor tracks and not
that hard, cement sidewalk. BUTTOCKS are firm because you're
exercising on a regular basis. The ASSHOLE is tight, and free of
VENEREAL WARTS. In fact, you've NEVER BEEN IN BET-
TER SHAPE. Some of you have CHOSEN TO BE FAT, because
FAT looks HEALTHY. Others have kept your TEENSY WAIST.
You're working out now BECAUSE YOU ENJOY IT. Because
EVEN WHEN WE STOP HAVING PICKUP SEX, we remain
as *vain* and *eroticized* as ever! FEET Now are in top condition,
and used only in J.O. scenes, or on brisk walks through the
woods overlooking the Hudson. BONUS: Massage your feet at
home—SENSUOUS and STRESS-DISSOLVING. BONUS:
Take your feet on a hiking tour of the Catskills. (But NOT Co-
pacabana Beach or the streets of Paris. Travel is part of Feet NOW
but not SEX VACATION—because some diseased QUEEN less
ethical than you has been there already and infected the locals!)
STOMACHS—unless you've decided to become a Porker—are
WASHBOARD. NIPPLES are SUBDUED. GENITALS—
bleached in Clorox—are worn UNOBTRUSIVELY. The INSIDE
OF YOUR RECTUM, in fact the entire LOWER COLON, re-
flects your decision to maintain SPATIAL INTEGRITY. They
have also been helped by your emphasis on *whole-grain* cereals
mixed with the RAW OATS found in those *divine* bins at your

favorite health food store. (STOOLS *float* on the surface because you are eating sufficient roughage.) CONSIDER: Macrobiotic. BONUS: Claims are made it can *bring your T-cell count back to normal.* FACT: You love CHOCOLATE CAKE. (And CHOCO-LATE is more important than ever this fall because you have nixed certain other forms of *oral gratification.*) BASIC: Whichever way you go, foundation *must be* a BALANCED, NATURAL DIET of fresh fruit and raw veggies. KEY: FART FOOD is GOOD FOOD because people who fart unpredictably, and often, are *not* going to risk the HUMILIATION entailed in blowing several hundred cubic feet of STALE GAS during a *let-yourself-go* orgasm. They STAY HOME MORE where they can fart to their heart's content! Use this EXTRA TIME to do KNEE EXERCISES—like *genuflection.* Memorize: "My Body Is the Temple of the Holy Ghost." *Keep it Clean.* With knees, feet, asshole, stomach in PERFECT SHAPE, your body HUMS, and a perfectly working BODY has always been, and is again this fall, the most important, crucial, fundamental element in—

Fashion NOW. Fashion, dressing, because of your totally new situation, *no longer present problems.* BONUS: Kiss good-bye hours wasted in your INSECURE SEX YEARS trying on T-shirts. (As if there was a *magic* T-shirt! As if there was a Mister Right!) The *despair* you felt after a night in the bars when you realized your outfit was NOT WORKING! Those DEGRADING afternoons spent with people MUCH younger than you in CANAL JEANS looking for pants that showed your ASS off! Your ASS *is in great shape, darling,* because it's WART-FREE! (For the longest time *ever.*) In Fall '85, you are not dressing to show your Body off. (Unless you're a sadist; and that's for ANOTHER COLUMN, dear.) You are dressing to be APPROPRIATE, UNNOTICED, COMFORTABLE, RELAXED. So BE CREATIVE. Fashion NOW is revolutionary because it no longer has to be validated by someone *unzipping his pants.* WHY? Because you're off FAST-FOOD SEX. It was thrilling, *of course.* But it wasn't doing your BODY any good. Junk food never does, darling. And it's FABULOUS now to know you won't be down on your KNEES over the next bimbo who walks through the door. Think of this Fall as a SEX BREAK. Think of the *New Celibacy* as a *Holiday,* a *Moment for Reflection.* Use this OPPORTUNITY to retrench, rededicate yourself to Old Ideals (which are JUST LIKE Old Clothes, darling: You can always pull them out of storage TEN YEARS LATER because EVERYTHING ALWAYS comes back! Look at NEW WAVE!). Use your OLD IDEALS to get out of TOWN, close to NATURE, read the DIVINE COMEDY, listen to ALL OF BARTOK straight through! Start writing that long-lost cousin in Sandusky, Ohio, who goes to church twice a week, is an aide in a nursing home, lifts weights, and has never even been SUNBURNED! Learn how to be a SUPERB *voyeur.* Or—if you know you'll never be able to DO WITHOUT *indefinitely*— come to grips with the NEW REALITY. Buy a package of LUXURIOUS CONDOMS and become familiar with them at home. Then INVITE FRIENDS over and give each one of *them* a package. DISCUSS your feelings about the Icky things (the Only Way you'll be able to have ANY SEX AT ALL in the coming years, dear) as you pass them around the table. Blow them up to wear as party hats. PARTY GAME: Try putting them on in record time. (Winner gets two tickets to *Cats*.) Learn to overcome your distaste, embarrassment, shyness, and hesitation about using them, or even SUGGESTING they be used to a prospective husband. Remember, darling, YOU HAVE NO CHOICE. It's raincoats or *nothing* so long as the skies are POURING DOWN VIRUSES. Be SMART. BEHAVE, dear heart. Use this *incredible* time to develop your—

Attitude NOW. *What people are reading, seeing, talking about.* The Chinese are going ahead with the FOUR MODERNIZATIONS, darling, and SO MUST WE. This fall you're WATCHFUL, WORRIED, HOPEFUL, SAD, REALISTIC, DEPRESSED, TENSE, CALM, ANXIOUS, ELATED, APPREHENSIVE, DETERMINED, BURSTING WITH ENERGY AND AFRAID TO USE IT. Let's face it: You're CONFUSED. You've never been so BESET with CONTRADICTORY MESSAGES. You want to be CALM, but you're really NERVOUS. You want to be COMPOSED, but you're actually UPSET. You've never felt SO ALIVE and never before been so CONSCIOUS OF THE PERILS involved in LIFE. You live in a culture SATURATED with COME-ONS, a society that PUTS A PREMIUM ON BEING ATTRACTIVE, but there is cancer in the air! You move through a city where you'd like to sleep with TEN MEN on every block, but you just don't know *which ones* are LETHAL. You're told by one set to make your body DROP DEAD, and by another NOT TO USE IT for any of those things that relieve our awful SOLITUDE. If years ago you were alienated from the world because of your homosexuality,

NOW you're alienated from *homosexuality*! Some are understandably in a state of HIBERNATION. You're looking for a MIDDLE ROAD. The way we see it: The Oil Glut ended, and so has the SEX GLUT. And *you're* left with the hangover. But you know we recovered from the ENERGY CRISIS and we can get through the LOVE CATASTROPHE. What to do? Press your HOLD Button. You know the NEW SOBRIETY, darling, can be a FABULOUS OPPORTUNITY. To ask just what IS going on. And how you want the FUTURE to be. Form small groups of CLOSE FRIENDS for Discussion and Consciousness-Enrichment. (Divine Henry James said, "Consciousness is everything." Isn't it, just.) BE REALISTIC. Ask yourself, *What would happen if the plague stopped tomorrow?* If the folks who brought us Pearl Harbor and the SONY Walkman found a cure *Tuesday?* BE HONEST: Everyone would start *slurping* again. (*Our Mouths, Ourselves.*) The gay newspapers you've been reading faithfully since this started would fill up with articles on BUTT-PLUGS. People would start getting *snotty* again about rejection and selection. *It wouldn't take much for us all to become junkies again!* But you're *aware* of that. *And too smart to let it happen!* You want to use this time to change your WHOLE APPROACH. Because, darling, when the plague ends—whenever!—and the papers DO drag out those *in-depth* features on Art Nouveau cock rings, and the man blows his whistle and yells, "*Que la fête commence!*," we want you to be just a LITTLE DIFFERENT. *Isn't that what being GAY is all about?* And until that happens—if the detail, *detail*, DETAIL of these endless precautions is just too much for you—then THINK BIG as you make your plans to get through this. Call the Whitney Museum, *ask for the Director*—don't be intimidated by Authority!—and tell him you'd like him to commission CHRISTO (the artist who put sheets all over those TINY islands in Biscayne Bay, and WANTED to do the paths in Central Park) to WRAP YOU. That, darling, will solve everything and make *you* WHAT PEOPLE ARE TALKING ABOUT this fall—the *best*, most *exciting*, and *terrifying* fall of your lives! Autumn in New York! Why does it set the heart DANCING? Because this year, my darlings, you are living on the EDGE. And we want you to maintain your BALANCE.

Next month: SHOPPING.

My Little Trojan

O F HOMOSEXUAL MEN not in monogamous pairs in New York
these days, there seem to be three sorts: the abstinent, the sex
junkie, and the worried sick. Our man belonged to the latter class
the day he walked into the drugstore on Sixth Avenue to purchase
contraceptives. The abstinent—having decided to have no sex at
all—do not have to purchase rubbers; the occasion to use one will
never arise. The sex junkie is still slurping away at the baths. The
worried sick are worried about AIDS because they know they cannot sustain chastity with the surprising ease of some of their
friends. They go to the baths and watch the sex junkies slurp but
do nothing themselves; they lust after men on the street and keep
walking; they form jack-off clubs, if they are practical, and
if they are not, periodically succumb to strangers. After doing this
they cannot sleep, however, wondering if this was the fatal trick. So
one day they walk into a drugstore on Sixth Avenue with a friend
and ask the clerk for rubbers, as the doctors have advised them to do.

The first rubber our hero ever saw was floating like a dead jellyfish against the shore of the Charles River in Boston one night in 1964. At the time, a student taking a break from his books, he associated rubbers with teenagers screwing in the backseats of cars in *Peyton Place*. They connoted the fifties as much as sex. Years later, he wondered why homosexual men didn't use them—if only because the sheathing ceremony seemed to dramatize the penis; and homosexuals were always trying to dramatize the penis. One homosexual friend told him rubbers were associated with women and that was why they weren't used. Another said, "Having sex with a rubber is like taking a shower in a raincoat." But still he was perplexed. Given the ceremony of draping the phallus, of turning it into a plastic dildo, why didn't the men who used cock rings use these too? Why had the man he'd seen at the Hothouse one night in San Francisco covered his bed with more tubes, coils, and metal instruments than could possibly be needed for a coronary bypass operation, or the castration of Chance Wayne in *Sweet Bird of Youth*—but no rubbers? In all those years since he spotted his first miserable used specimen, for whatever reason, condoms had been disdained by homosexual men.

So it feels strange for our protagonist to be walking into the drugstore on Sixth Avenue that day with a friend to purchase prophylactics—not to prevent pregnancy (the reason the Catholic Church forbids them), to prevent death. When he first heard on the radio that doctors suspected sperm might carry cancer, he thought it must be a fantasy of the religious right. But here he is now, asking the clerk to show them the condoms—lubricated, ribbed, plain—displayed on a shelf above them: various brands at various prices. He chooses a box of Trojans that cost approximately fifty cents a condom; neither the least nor the most expensive. The box is blue and has a photograph of a man and a woman on the beach—in love, about to be attacked by a seagull.

The friends laugh as they leave the store, but he thinks that with these condoms, his life has totally changed. Armed with six Trojans, he has found a way around the sexual block which has turned New York into a nightmare. The future is now manageable. He intends to carry one at all times, like a Boy Scout with his Boy Scout knife. He is now safe. The rubber in his pants pocket is like a crucifix in a land of vampires. It is a quarter to be put in a slot machine, or the dime he was given as a child to go out and buy a Good Humor bar; he can exchange it for sex. My little Trojan, he thinks, means I can trick again. One Trojan, one trick. He knew life did not have to be so dreary!

Then the cultural, psychological, social reality sets in—because he doesn't know quite how to introduce the thing. He is polite. The first time he uses the rubber, his partner is a man celebrating a clean bill of health by going to the baths. (These are odd, schizophrenic times.) The stranger is too involved with his own feelings to notice him slip the rubber on, surreptitiously, like a burglar putting on gloves to crack a safe. The encounter goes well enough and our protagonist is proud of himself. A week later, however, he is so excited he does not stop to use the rubber—he doesn't want to interrupt the crescendo of lust—and when our hero mentions afterward that he had planned to use a condom, his partner looks at him and says, "I would have been insulted."

"Why?" our hero says. "It's not that I think you're diseased, but *I* may be, or either one of us. Who knows? A condom protects us both."

Things go downhill from there. Our hero asks his next trick to use a rubber, and together they watch his penis shrivel. The next man refuses to even consider it. The third one agrees by saying, "Sure. If you eat what's in it afterwards."

Our hero is insecure enough already—he hasn't the confidence of his friend, who tells him he waits till his partner is so excited it doesn't matter, and even claims that it delights young people when he brings it out. "Oh! A scumbag!" they gasp. "I've never seen one!"

Our hero soon loses his initial sense of enchantment, however—and before very long he has learned why people do not want to use the things. The reason is simple: In the midst of pleasure, the rubber recalls disease, danger, death, his own friends' illness. Its use is prudent, rational, sensible. But sex is a surrender to what is not prudent, rational, sensible. It is the escape from these. In the heat of lust—generated by small concessions that are themselves rational—he loses his resolve.

So by the time he goes home, on a sex vacation, with someone in San Francisco who puts his own brand of condoms—Ramses—on the table by the bed, he has become entirely weary of the subject. (Ramses was a pharaoh, he thinks, but these things remind me of Saran Wrap.) It was nice that he did not to have to bring the subject up, but as his partner prepares himself in the bathroom, he stares glumly at the condoms on the tabletop the way he looks at the little circle of dental instruments next to his face when he goes to have his teeth worked on. Then he examines his own little Trojan on the bedside table. By now its blue package is worn and frayed. He has carried it around so long, changed it from pants pocket to pants pocket, that he wonders if its sanitary integrity is not compromised—by a tear in the lining. (This is the objection his chaste friends have to rubbers: "Rubbers can break!") Tears in the lining, he reminds himself, are what this is all about, so he puts a new Trojan in his pocket when he gets home.

It sits there, a sop to his conscience and little else, since after his return from San Francisco he stops tricking. He suspects he will never use his rubber. When he is rational enough to use it, he is rational enough to resist sex; and when he is so horny he does not care, he can resist nothing. The blue Trojan can be used only in between these states, but between these poles (of abstinence and debauch, fear and recklessness) he no longer exists. He is either Doctor Jekyll or Mister Hyde. He cannot arrange sex the way he arranges a trip to the beach.

Months after leaving the drugstore on Sixth Avenue, our hero knows the most effective weapon isn't the rubber in his pocket— Fear is. Fear forms a barrier between him and the man he cruises who keeps walking because both of them are potentially diseased meat. Then one night—after weeks of Fear—he rebels, and visits the baths with his rubber, just to see men. He is so certain he won't have sex he leaves the rubber in the locker downstairs. (How does one carry one anyway when wearing just a towel; pinched between the fingers, like a Handiwipe, or a package of peanuts the stewardess offers you on the airplane?) And then upstairs—as quickly as a spark turns a dry hillside into a wall of fire—he makes a mistake. The joke is right: A stiff cock has no conscience. It has no brains, either. He goes home afterward to such recrimination and worry, he lies awake till dawn—feeling the prophylactic of terror tighten about him.

It comes down to this, he thinks, in these peculiar times: a problem of custom, of usage, of marketing. Getting homosexuals to accept rubbers will be like getting fifty million rural housewives in India fitted for IUDs. Nothing can compete with a naked dick.

Except Fear, of course—next time he'll try harder, he thinks. Next time he'll use his Trojan, which sits meekly on his bedside table, more honored in the breach than the observance. Dawn brightens the bricks of the wall outside his window. He looks at the condom—the bright flag of his disposition, his constant pal, the worry beads he has carried with him for six months now, half in reason, half in superstition—and decides to put it on. "My little Trojan," he thinks. "I might as well use you by myself, since I'm probably not going to use you when I'm with someone else." It unwraps down from its little ring, like the train of an Italian princess in the fifteenth century, encasing the penis in a sheath as thin as filo dough, opaque and clinical in color. It's not pretty. He smiles at the sight of himself: lying in bed with his rubber on, like a fireman suited up, or a man in a gas mask waiting for an air raid. Then he takes it off, and removes another from the box and puts that one on the table. "Good night," he says as he closes his eyes and waits for sleep to end the confusion of his day. "Sleep tight, my little Trojan."

Ground Zero

THE METROPOLITAN THEATRE—though one never used the second word, so that when you told someone where you were going, it might have been the Museum or the Opera— is no longer as dark as it used to be. The two long hallways running down either side of the ground floor are brightly lighted now, and the foyer downstairs is actually visible. In the seventies the darkness of the Metropolitan was legendary; to walk into this decrepit theater on Fourteenth Street and Second Avenue was to enter a deep black cave in which it was impossible to see anything— that was the point—but now, in March 1987, the strictures of safer sex have resulted, even here, in brighter lightbulbs, and the place seems small.

Much about New York seems small to me now, however—as if the whole city has shrunk to a single fact. I wander around the city, past the buildings going up on Third Avenue, the crowds on Fifth, aware that inside the external aggrandizement of the city's power and glitter is another, smaller city that haunts the mind as a sort of doppelgänger. The city as cemetery. When I come home to New York now, I go straight to one of the movie houses showing pornographic films near my apartment on the Lower East Side. At the end of a day spent visiting friends in hospital rooms—intelligent, brave, accomplished men breathing oxygen through tubes, staring at a brick wall outside the window—when I get down to the street, my instinct is to run, not walk, straight through this earthly hell to the Metropolitan and, once its doors close behind me, relax; relax in the comfort of the very thing that has become the Siamese twin of death. After leaving the hospital room of the friend whose pancreas has ceased to function, after leaving the apartment of the young man going blind, after meeting on the sidewalk a thirty-six-year-old acquaintance who looks eighty-nine, I walk through the cold, crowded city or down a deserted street to one of these doorways and obliterate everything in the dark, warm chamber of seed. Nothing else provides the comfort this place does—no other experience.

There is something sad, delicious, and infinitely erotic about these movie houses now that in the past seemed merely sordid. The Metropolitan has always been here—it still even costs the same three dollars—but it depressed me in the seventies; I must have gone there two times the entire decade. Often I walked by it. Passing the Metropolitan, I always thought of a story by Tennessee Williams called "The Mysteries of the Joy Rio," about a dirty old man in the balcony of a dirty old movie house. The Metropolitan was synonymous with sleaze—famous for mixing a clientele that consisted of successful models from the Upper East Side with residents of the Lower East Side; one of those places where two groups that did not meet often socially could meet in the dark. It was so dark one could hardly see any of the men lining the hallways, the balconies, the stage behind the movie screen—and all I remember now is the feeling one had standing in the lobby, buttoning one's coat, before going back out onto the street: that dull, depressed feeling of failure, of dejection—at having to rejoin a world in which light, law, manners, reality kept one at a distance from the objects of one's erotic dreams. Sometimes I would walk afterward across Union Square to a bathhouse that only cost three dollars, too. But now the baths are closed. Despite the fact that they are a sensible environment for the practice of safe sex, the Hassidim picketed the one on my block, the courts acted, and its black doors are shut. A few remain—on Wall Street, in Harlem—but they don't seem worth the trouble; in middle age, one prefers what is closer to home. And the Metropolitan is a five-block walk from my apartment, one block farther than the Jewel.

My urge to run here immediately upon returning to New York is fueled by not very mysterious things—the reasons people go to these places in ordinary times: loneliness and lust. But it's also a response to the fact that New York is no longer a city one returns to anymore with the exhilaration and joy that used to make one consider kneeling down on the airport tarmac, like the pope, and kissing the ground upon arrival at Newark. New York is the center of the epidemic, where you learn almost inevitably that another friend is sick or see those who already are, knowing all the while you cannot do anything but behave as well as possible and wonder if they hate you for not being there with them. Depression is what brings me to the pornographic movie house—the same way it sent me home from the hospital the autumn I spent visiting a relative in intensive care (among the nurses, tubes, machinery, and horror), to turn the TV on to *Mister Rogers' Neighborhood,* because he was so soothing, simple, and calm. There is an urge, when life seems totally crushing, to just crawl back into the womb.

And the womb is what these theaters—the Metropolitan, the Adonis, the Jewel—seem to me now: dark and quiet and calm. They are, moreover, all that is left, it seems, of homosexuality. Or at least one aspect of it: the central one. "I don't know anyone who's gay anymore," says a woman I know. "Gay is not an option." The bars, the discotheques, that are still open seem pointless in a way; the social contract, the assumptions, that gave them their meaning are gone. They turn you serious, if you stay long enough—because every bar, every dance floor, reminds you eventually of a friend. The memory of friends is everywhere. It pervades the city. Buildings, skylines, corners have holes in them—gaps: missing persons. And if the present is a cemetery, the future is a minefield. I think sometimes that if, in the old days, over a long enough period of time, everyone had slept with everyone else, one might now say, "Over a long enough period of time, everyone is diagnosed." The pitier becomes the pitied eventually. As one man said after being diagnosed, "I wasn't doing anything everyone else wasn't." Exactly.

Years ago, when the first friend died, those he'd left behind talked about his illness for months; the whole city seemed haunted by him; we could not imagine New York without Eddie. Now when the news comes that the twenty-fifth or thirty-ninth friend has died, I discuss the death, and before hanging up the phone, ask the person who brings these tidings if he wants to go to the movies Tuesday. It's nearly banal. Won't someone please turn off the bubble machine? We get the point. The friend who lives upstate says calling friends in Manhattan is "like phoning Germany in the thirties." Or, as a friend who lives in town puts it, "It's like living in Beirut. You never know where the next bomb is going to go off." The bomb seems the best metaphor as I wander the Metropolitan. "Oh," people say when they learn someone left New York in 1983, "you got out before the bomb fell." Well, not really, he wants to reply, the bomb fell several years before that. Only we didn't know it. The bomb fell without anyone's knowing the bomb had fallen, which is how it destroyed a community that now seems—looking back—as extinct as the Mayans.

The Mayans left temples in the Yucatán; we seem to have left pornography. At the Jewel—around the corner—they show films in which the actors are all men; the first time I went there I sat for hours watching them, the way one might watch a movie about Chichén Itzá. It seemed—this sunny Californian world that provided our sexual icons—as distant from the present as life upon the pyramids of ancient Yucatán, divided from the present—in both cases—by a single cataclysmic fact. People go to the Jewel not only to watch the films, however. They go to cruise, to breathe the forbidden atmosphere. What persists through all this is the allure of the body. "The skin," a man at the Jewel explained, when we left together in a cab, "needs to be touched." (His apartment, on the other hand, was littered with three-by-five cards on which he'd written, BHAGWAN, PLEASE PROTECT ME FROM AIDS. We ended up talking, not touching—the exchange of stories, of fear, that sometimes replaces sex itself.)

At the Metropolitan—for a reason I never understood fully—the mostly gay audience watches (or does not watch) heterosexual fantasies on-screen. That is part of the mystique, the legend, of the Metropolitan—the illusion that this place was more *real*. Now things are too real, of course, and the Metropolitan seems fantastic. The women in black lingerie, garters, and stockings produce a cascade of fervid gasps, an "Oh! Oh! Oooooh!" in the backseat of automobiles, a tent overlooking Big Sur, a train compartment, that makes one think men do not even come close to enjoying sex, that only women experience pleasure. The men attending them on-screen seem merely drones—as nervous and harried as bank robbers pulling off a job. The men in the audience sit for the most part alone—straight men, perhaps, who don't care what the rest of the audience is doing, or men whose egos require that they establish their masculinity by watching women first, or simply men who need the time to adjust their eyesight to the darkness and to figure out just what is going on and who is here.

Who is here are mostly black and Hispanic men. The graffiti in the hallway reads, among other things, STOP NIGGERS FROM SPREADING AIDS and PUERTO RICANS RULE. Fifty-three percent of the cases in New York City are now Hispanic and black (which has more to do with drugs than with homosexuality and more to do—most cruelly—with babies than with right or wrong). For a while, blacks thought it was a white man's disease, and whites thought blacks had caused it: Africa accusing Europe, and Europe accusing Africa. Everyone wants someone else to have AIDS, if someone has to have it. Farther down the wall in the same handwriting are the words EVEN A SIMPLE BLOW JOB CAN GIVE YOU AIDS. USE RUBBERS AND LIVE! (Most gay men do not believe this; they think oral sex is safe.) Rubbers are something one was once embarrassed to even suggest—at the beginning—for fear one would be considered anal-compulsive, neurotic, germophobic. Rubbers were jokes, the idea of constraints on sex anathema to those who argued that the essence of sex was freedom, and the glory of freedom sex. "He said he'd use a rubber," one friend told me, "if I'd eat what was in it afterward." Safety ran counter to the whole expansive spirit of the seventies, the exhilarating suspicion that we were pioneers in the pursuit of human happiness and no one had found its limits yet. The plague provided limits. Limits that seemed so draconian and harsh that even after their arrival—during that period when people knew, but did not quite believe—friends considered infringements on their sexual options to be merely more American puritanism. There was no romance in rational sex. (The curious paradox of anonymous sex, of one-night stands, of places like the Metropolitan, was their deeply romantic nature.) The death of Dionysus—the closing down of promiscuity—took a long time to complete itself, a lot of fear. But fear was what the plague has produced copiously, till it now constitutes the substance of homosexual life. AIDS has been a massive form of aversion therapy. For if you finally equate sex with death, you don't have to worry about observing safe-sex techniques; sex itself will eventually become unappetizing. And the male body will turn into an object of dread—not joy—an object whose touch makes you lie awake afterward, with the suspicion you have just thrown your life away for a bit of pleasure. "There's so much more to life than sex," says a friend who has sworn off it for several years now. "What?" I say. "Well, living," he says. "Living is important to life." Yet despite this—because of this—we come to the Metropolitan.

I come to the Metropolitan for the same reason friends began traveling to Brazil when the plague began—escape. But standing there letting my eyes adjust to the darkness, I cannot help but think of friends who are not there with me—seeing what I see. Life's a movie people leave at different times; the ones who remain get to see a little more of what happens next. Eddie and I used to see things together—now I come here alone. "I'm going to Ceil's for lunch, then the D&D Building, then down to your neighborhood for a shiatsu massage from that Dutch boy, and then I thought I'd drop by the Metropolitan," he'd call and say, reciting a menu for the afternoon that only a city like New York can offer. "I'll wait for you before going in. It's only three dollars!" It was much more expensive than that—but we didn't know this when we met on the sidewalk in a lightly falling snow that dusted the mustaches of the young Puerto Ricans passing the glass doors of the theater that separated the public from the private world. Eddie usually wore his torn fatigues and ripped tank top, under an Armani topcoat. His motto was Auntie Mame's: "Life's a banquet, and most poor fools are starving to death." Eddie's not here now. Other people are. They wander back and forth—across the foyer, up and down the aisles, searching, searching.

Sometimes we forget how far we've come, or at least how much we have assimilated, in the past four years. The shock is gone now, perhaps, the dangers accommodated in daily life. Each person makes his daily wager with the facts. The telephone still strikes a residual fear each time it rings—it will bring, for sure, more bad news—but it's not what it used to be: the panic of a shark attack. Yet the sadism, the cruelty, the meanness of the disease, remain the same. It may no longer surprise, but it still takes the breath away—and makes you yearn for an end to the suffering. "I keep thinking there's a beach at the end of this," a friend said. "An island, and we'll be happy again." In the meantime, I come to the Metropolitan the moment I get back to Fun City.

And it is fun—the old freedom, the old romance, the old excitement, come back the moment the doors to the lobby close behind me, and, after allowing my eyes to adjust to the darkness, I start to walk around. There may be far fewer vignettes—people have adapted; they always do—but there are still some. Two men squat downstairs on toilets in the bathroom stalls, cans of beer lined up in a row at their feet, peeking out around the partitions to see who's coming, with the expression of children waiting for Santa Claus. When the plague began, and I heard stories of people with AIDS having sex with others without telling them till it was over, I thought them preposterous; now, given the depression, the despair, the idea that what-the-world-gave, I-can-give-back, I believe them all. The prostitutes with AIDS who keep going back to work exemplify a strain in everyone. The best guide to this mysterious battleground in which death may be entirely hidden was given by a friend with AIDS: "Treat everyone as if they have it." Caveat emptor. That really is all people need. No legislation is necessary. The Metropolitan seems so dangerous that it's safe. When I go upstairs again, I notice that most men watching the movie sit alone in their seats—alone and safe—but others are walking back and forth along the dark rear walls that lead up to the balconies. Even there, at the darkest center of the Metropolitan, the men leaning against the wall of the projection booth are separate. No clumps, no orgies; none of the feeding frenzies that, even before the plague, made one wonder what it all meant. In the darkest corner, the handsomest Puerto Rican in the place—so far—is being licked by someone I cannot see. Next, a handsome youth who looks as if he just got off the bus from Indiana comes up the stairs, can of beer in hand; his bright eyes, broad-shouldered frame, wide-open expression (what does it mean?) are the image of health, the look cereal companies use in commercials. He walks onto the narrow balcony, sits down next to a black man who is leaning against the wall, and stares at him . . . the white man watching the black man, the black man watching the white woman on the screen . . . till the black man approaches his seat and there is a connection: like a car stopping at a gas tank, a bee on an azalea in spring. The mouth fits over the tube, the figures merge in silhouette, and a crowd gathers to watch what many of them will not do themselves anymore.

For if the plague is now part of everyone's information kit, the individual bargains people make with it are just that: entirely individual. Someday—not just yet—there will be novels about all of this, but they will face the problem writing about it stumbles against now: how to include the individual stories, the astonishingly various ways in which people have behaved. Downstairs, at the end of the hallway that runs the length of the theater, brightly lighted now, a handsome Puerto Rican stands before a man kneeling in a shadowy curve in the wall. As I watch, the Puerto Rican removes his penis from his pants and slaps it against the palm of his hand. It's a form of theater. When the man on his knees hobbles over to approach the penis, the Puerto Rican says, "No!" and glares at his supplicant, who then backs up and begins to masturbate, till the man on his knees in the corner ejaculates onto the floor. It lies there, like plutonium. "Thanks," he says, getting up. "You did this just right. You were terrific." He zips up his pants and adds, "Do you want a condom?" A token of thanks the Puerto Rican accepts from his admirer, who then leans against the door and falls out onto the street—the final testimony to this performance the fact that he can leave now, he has got what he came for, and needed. Ah, New York: always the same, ever new.

Cleaning My Bedroom

IT'S A TYPICAL East Village apartment—if there is such a thing: ceilings of average height, a big kitchen, a front room (which is really in the back of the building), short hallway with bathroom, and bedroom. The bedroom gets no light, and looks out at a brick wall about two feet away. It was the first apartment I had without a tub in the kitchen, however, and therefore has always seemed to me luxurious. When I moved in, I got all my furniture from the street—chairs with busted springs, et cetera—built shelves out of concrete blocks, and bookcases of metal milk crates. The paint was peeling off the walls and ceiling, there were roaches in the kitchen, the window in the bathroom was broken, and the bedroom dark—but it all worked, because it went with the neighborhood, and neither it nor I had any pretensions in matters of decor. The Frenchman I invited over one evening understood when he walked in: "Ah," he said, as he looked around, "*la vie bohème*." Friends called it the Tomb of Ligeia.

That's all it was for several years—until the roommate I acquired one year decided, the winter I was gone, to renovate the kitchen and the room he slept in. He hired a young carpenter-designer who transformed the two rooms into gleaming white simulacra of the photos published in the *New York Times*'s home section: sanded floors, Formica counters and cabinets, dimmers and ceiling-high bookcase. The detritus of the renovation was put in my bedroom: two-by-fours, plaster, discarded molding, manuscripts (in large, extra-strength trash bags), lamps and blenders, vegetable juicer, silverware, ceramic chotchkas for the kitchen no one ever used or threw out, bookends, phone books, phone table, headdresses worn to the Feather Ball, thrown in a heap in the back room. The carpenter who did the work never took down the old timbers and bags of plaster—the apartment is on the sixth floor—and when I returned, after the renovations were complete, and peeked around the bedroom door (which now opened only a crack), I was astonished by the proportions of the rubble. It seemed, curiously, to represent my own collapsed life in New York at that time: I was hardly there anymore, and since I never used the room for anything but sleep, and my roommate never used it at all, it seemed reasonable that it should remain a garbage dump. The timbers I took down, because nails were sticking out of them—and a few bags of plaster (though the bedroom ceiling periodically supplied more)—but I left everything else. Everything else was covered with dust, a fine gray-white dust: the towel hanging on a nail in the door, the green trash bags filled with manuscripts, the books on the windowsill, the windowsill, the suits and shirts hanging from a pole at the end of the room.

The sheets were mercifully covered with a comforter, though once I returned to find a dark stain of urine and heap of hardened cat turds on that: The cat, driven mad by a full litter box, had shat on my bed, using the room as her place of refuge, too. Even this did not compel me to clean the place out, however. I aired the comforter over the windowsill in the front room, shook the dust out of my towel, and continued my vacation. My vacations—those biannual visits to New York lasting a week or two—were so important to me I did not think it worth my time to clear the bedroom. I was only there to sleep, change clothes, use the phone.

Of course a bedroom is in fact used for much more than that—it's the temple of our psyches, the place in which we can shut out the world, make love, read, unwind, daydream, sleep, lie abed Sunday morning with the newspaper, close the door on the whole stressful, high-strung life that begins the moment you leave your house or apartment. It's a New Yorker's chief retreat; the place of last resort; the Cave of Somnus, the River of Lethe, the Temple of Eros. Once my bedroom had been a kind of shrine to which I brought back human gods—found, like my furniture, on the street (O wondrous city!). I would, like a good altar boy, light the candles, some fat, some thin, which lined the windowsill on glass saucers, to view that most holy object (the body) in their light. On such evenings—the door shut, the candles burning with still, upright flames in the windless air, the radiator pipe hissing, a man in bed beside me—this room was the most enchanted place in the world, or at least the very reason I lived in New York.

Now those days are past; one day years ago my roommate and I agreed not to bring people back to the apartment for sex, out of deference to each other; the plague began; and the candles that had illumined these sacred, paradisiacal, sometimes comic, sometimes depressing moments are now covered with dust themselves and sit unused, guttered, waxy, gnarled, on glass saucers so encrusted with ash and soot they seem made of another material. And I come home to bed now with merely the newspaper and an ice cream sandwich, to unplug the phone, stash it among the garbage bags, read the next day's headlines, and then turn off the light, falling asleep finally on mountains of junk—mountains of junk that, I realize now, made me feel as temporary, as uprooted, as depressed as most of the people I know in New York these past four years; afraid of the future, horrified by the present, not knowing what to think of the past.

And now that the sky itself seemed to have fallen in upon us, the plaster dust and shards, the heaps of unused objects that I climbed over to get to my bed, or the pole on which my shirts hung (embroidered now with ermine collars of dust) seemed perfectly true, right, appropriate, in tune with the times. The young man who did the renovation recently decided he loathed homosexuals and homosexual life, and no longer even speaks to my roommate when they pass on the street. My roommate's new friends, in turn, have nothing to do with his milieu in the seventies (gym, Saint, Fire Island); and his new life—macrocrobiotics, celibacy—seems to turn its back on the past with an almost surgical finality: Like Harriet Craig, he keeps his countertops, pots, and pans scrupulously clean in the new kitchen. Only the bathroom and short hall leading to my refuse-heaped bedroom remain in the premodern state. My roommate showers at his new gym, far, far from Sheridan Square, and does not use the bathroom much; it and the crummy hall outside seem to form a buffer zone, a transition period between his devotion to a New Age and my remaining in the Past.

The Past has exploded in our face like some car on a street corner in Lebanon. When I went out the door one morning to spend a day on Fire Island, he looked at me and cracked, "Don't be wistful!" But wistful was exactly how I planned to feel. When I found one afternoon a trove of photographs my roommate had taken during summers at the beach, I sat down and pored over them. They seemed at first as innocent as all photographs of summers at the beach: men lying on blankets under a cloudless blue Atlantic sky. The men were all muscular—so muscular their bodies seemed to have nothing to do with their much smaller heads. The handsomest was now dead. He lay on the blanket with four other men, bound together by some invisible witticism, their bodies curled with a laugh about to explode from their lips. The longer I looked—at the silver-sharp sunlight, the wide beach, the distant and irrecoverable laughter—the more extraordinary he seemed: free, stylish burnished by the sun; paragon of a way of life whose main sense of proportion had to do with muscle groups. But that was thought for some other time; on their face, the photos were so delightful, I put them on the kitchen table with a note for my roommate to find.

When I returned that evening and asked excitedly if he had seen the pictures, he looked across the two chopsticks suspending a strand of boiled seaweed at his lips and said, "I threw them out." "Why?" I asked. "Because I don't want to look at dead people," he said. "That's morbid." I did not say that was no reason to consign them to the trash—but that was his reaction to the horror; mine was to pick the packets of photos out of the garbage can and put them back in the bedroom, where they would presumably remain intact, in my Museum of the Past.

I had been removed from New York in 1983 through circumstances that had nothing to do with the plague—but now when I returned to Manhattan for those brief visits, I felt like the World War II veteran who returns home a stranger to his wife and children. The cat recognized me—I think—but my roommate did not; he told me which pots and pans I was to avoid (like kosher implements, reserved for macrobiotic cooking) and even left a frosty note one morning after he'd gone to work about my use of a forbidden frying pan the night before. All these things hurt. But his friends were dying; my friends were dying; and New York was merely a place where one went to funerals and avoided the eyes of other men on the street—at least, in our generation. The things on which we based our lives had proved disastrous. The rubble in my bedroom was no less than the rubble of our friendship, the rubble of homosexual life, the rubble of fear, the uncertainty, the impossible present and grimmer future. The cosmic transportation system must be very busy, a friend now living in San Francisco wrote one evening; there are so many trains taking away the dead; while reading the obituaries in the *Bay Area Reporter* in a restaurant on Haight Street, he burst into tears. Another writes at three in the morning from Seattle, because he is awake with diarrhea, about a new infection his doctor has just told him he has. I climb over the shards of plaster, dust, trash bags of failed novels, to reach my toothbrush, towel, and finally bed, and relax only when I shut the light off and plunge the whole room—like the letters, the place, the headlines of the *New York Post* about a man I know with AIDS jumping out the window of his apartment with his lover—into darkness.

It is not that life in New York has ended—young men walk down St. Marks Place at six o'clock on their way home from work with perfect haircuts and dreams as romantic as mine when I arrived in town. Friends still take shares in houses on Fire Island and give a party for their new housemates, and watching them— good-looking, giddy, hopeful—I am reminded that in this vast and various city, in the midst of the plague (or New Age, depending on your viewpoint), everything still goes on, somewhere. My roommate wants to forget everything about the Past; others I meet stop me, like the Ancient Mariner, to reminisce, starry-eyed, about people, parties, an era so free of care it seems to them mythical. And why not? We want the past five years to be a nightmare one wakes up from; we want it all to have been a bad dream and not something we will have to live, or die, with for the rest of our lives, like the fallout from Chernobyl. We want there to be a whistle, or siren, that signals "All Clear." Fear and hope come and go in alternating waves, prompted by the latest statistic, phone call, newscast, blood test. Conversations that begin on the old high note end in gloom. The homosexual world—its common language—is broken up now. There are many dialects. Many conditions—some sick, some well, some with reason to worry, others with none. It's as eclectic as life in New York: in any crowd walking down St. Marks Place, young men in business suits carrying attaché cases, skinheads with great prongs of hair radiating from their scalps, fifties haircuts on Elvis Presley profiles, boys who want to look like Japanese art students in Paris, men with the long hair and pony tails I last saw in the sixties, and—a small fraction of what used to be the cutting edge— museum-quality clones in mustaches and jeans. The city is all jumbled up. The ghetto has blurred, unraveled, like the sexuality of individual gay men. Friends of mine, turning homophobic, say they're attracted only to straight men or women; when they look at homosexuals, they think of death. The Saint—that cathedral of the seventies—is now desanctified; friends who went there with religious fervor now go to a Sufi dance class. I cannot tell who is gay or straight in the East Village, and when I go to the bars, I have no sense of the mood of the man across the room. It is probably like mine: bedeviled, frustrated, and cautious. Yet at the Palladium you can still dance to "Golden Oldies"—the cream of disco from the seventies—in a nest of Puerto Ricans in muscle shirts and dark glasses who are obviously drugged. The floor is jammed with gym bodies. But when "Love's Theme" comes on, and I look up to remember the dead friend who loved this song ("Listen to the violins going up, up, up!" he used to say), a huge volleyball net descends from the ceiling and an enormous balloon, which the dancers hit back and forth across it. So much for remembrance. So much for trying to draw a line between the past and the present. There is no clear boundary between the two.

Though I may ask myself, *What would X be doing today if he were alive?* and, *How would gay life have evolved had there been no plague?*, the answers would be meaningless. He's not, and there was, and that's that. And these reflections somehow—over the course of a night's sleep—produce the next morning, when I awaken, a decision to clean my bedroom.

It is one of those tasks you do by not stopping to plan—by saying aloud, "Don't think about it. Just start with that pile." The papers I touch send up clouds of dust that make me sneeze, the heaps look insurmountable, but I go ahead because I want, for the first time in four years, to walk on the floor. I have not walked on the floor in four years because I've been intimidated by the proportions of this rubble, but now I pick up all the dusty, dirty clothes and take them to the laundry on Second Avenue; then excavate the rest—jackets, sweaters, bathing suits, parkas, boots, sweatshirts, jeans, books, letters, bank statements, travel brochures, schedules of ferries to Fire Island, Long Island Railroad timetables to Sayville and Freeport, a pool schedule for the McBurney YMCA, two tennis rackets, an old passport, a cash machine credit card that is no good, old running shoes stiff with dust, pornographic magazines, a collage of photographs I'd composed on a piece of cardboard linking nude men I thought belonged together, an invitation, stamped on a coaster, to a Wild West party at the River Club—the archeological evidence of a life that seems to have been unable to locate a golden mean between Trivia and Catastrophe. Then I find my journal, caked with dust. The journal—when I open it and choose an entry at random—

reminds me again of the friend I thought of the previous night on hearing that song by Barry White and the Love Unlimited Orchestra. On 5/22/74:

"The Island: Running along the beach in the Pines from Water Island, the sun on the sea, that feeling—sitting by the pool with T. after ham sandwich and beer—carpenters hammering all around—Rosa stoned in the bus house, getting packed, singing, 'My man loves my big dick, and the bigger it gets the more he likes it.'"

The first person is alive; the second is dead, but he lives again, completely, in that bawdy song. The other entries reflect the same dichotomy. I read a few more descriptions: of sex partners, trips to San Francisco, Fire Island; and then put it aside for the moment, open a drawer and pick up several guest passes to a gym I no longer belong to; a dusty slide of a man I thought the handsomest on Fire Island in the early seventies; a tube of Bain de Soleil 6 (we now prefer 15; the sun is considered as lethal as sperm); a checkbook I thought I'd lost; the metallic ruler with which I measured my penis after I moved to New York and learned that these dimensions mattered; bottles of moisturizer; a squash racket with a broken string; Rilke's *Letters to a Young Poet*; Freud's *Civilization and Its Discontents*; an invitation to an exhibit of a friend's architectural drawings, from August 20 to September 15, 1983, at a gallery in Southampton. (Can George be dead only two years? It seems much longer.) In the same heap of papers the invitation is in, I find a plastic sandwich bag in which two white quaaludes and a shattered, pale blue valium lie. Quaaludes: relaxation of the sphincter, the languorous erotic surrender forbidden now. What would I do if I took these quaaludes now—yoga? I put them in a drawer, pick up a scrap of paper, which I read and try to make sense of: *Michael Greenberg, Sweeney Todd (tire store), Christopher Street.* What does that mean? My bedroom is half cleared, and I put the scraps in a basket on the chest of drawers, sexual confetti, in a wicker Out box. Then I pick up the old issue of *Honcho* (April 1979). Inside is a long article on fisting by James Henry—celebratory, informative, upbeat. A doctor is interviewed. The author closes with a recollection of one of his "best experiences ever. Two lovers, both into fisting, both with magnificent, talented holes. We did a threesome on an outdoor waterbed on Fire Island, in the middle of the afternoon." He speculates about the future: "It is possible, given our sophistication and jadedness, that such an esoteric practice . . . will someday be the norm for homosexual men. . . . Or perhaps sexual heads, and the trips that go along with them, are subject to change and evolution." (You bet.)

"We may all wind up back in a heavily oral stage . . . we may wind up tripping out on ourselves in elaborate multimedia jerk-off trips. Others say we'll be into asexuality." (How prescient!)

"Who knows? Whether fisting is here to stay, or just the hit of the seventies, I'm glad I'll be able to tell my hypothetical grand-children what it was like when fisting was young." *When fisting was young*—it seems, this jaunty piece, like a letter written by someone in the lounge of the *Titanic*: "Having a wonderful crossing, the food is superb, Father and I are just about to go down to dinner." (Crash.)

Emmanuel's Loft

WE MET IN 1979—shortly after he'd moved from San Francisco to New York. He was a correspondent for the French newspaper *Gai Pied*, and wanted to talk to me about a novel I had written. We sat on a park bench in Washington Square. After our conversation, he closed the little notebook, put away his pen, looked straight ahead and said, with the air of someone taking inventory, "You are my first friend in New York." I was both touched and taken aback—we had only spent an hour together, and I wondered how this could be construed as friendship. But then sometimes an hour, a first meeting, feels like that. Of course, we often wonder why a person likes us, and I asked that question almost immediately after meeting Emmanuel. I concluded that it was simply because I'd written a book about a New York milieu he was interested in—a milieu I was tired of at that point (the world of discos, and Fire Island), but which he, a newcomer to Manhattan, a foreigner, found glamorous. Dreams are like revolving doors, I'd written in my novel—someone is always coming into the one you are going out of. Emmanuel had written a study of the gay ghetto in San Francisco called *La Société Invertie*, but New York, Fire Island, the dance clubs of Manhattan, were all new to him.

He had a bony face, with a shock of blond hair hanging over his forehead. He sometimes wore bow ties, and smoked little thin cheroots that, cocked at an angle, gave him the air of a dandy. Was his hair dyed? Did he toss it with a certain affectation, as he held his cigarillo? Did he care about the newest restaurant, movie, book, too much? It didn't bother me, because both of us were observers who loved to exchange impressions, particularly of people.

There were a lot of people in Emmanuel's life. I worked at home, nearly a recluse. Emmanuel seemed to require a large cast of characters. He had a French wife with whom he had traveled all around the world. He had a lover named Jorge, a best friend named Jean Michel, and a clique consisting of an astonishingly handsome Brazilian and two crazies named Antonio and Patricio, one Spanish, one Argentine. New York seemed to be simply where Emmanuel had alighted for the moment. Born in Egypt, raised in Indochina, he had set out with his wife, after his parents retired to France, to India and Yemen and San Francisco. He had written his book on San Francisco while living in Rio de Janeiro. In New York he got a job translating at the United Nations. He had no desire to live in Paris—his best friend, Jean Michel, had given up Paris too, for Montreal; they both seemed to hold French people in contempt, even though Emmanuel had gone to school at the Sorbonne and written his thesis on Proust. (He said he had learned more about life by reading Proust than through any other source. Proust formed a common text, with which we could turn to one another and compare someone to Madame de Verdurin, or Bloch.) At any rate, Emmanuel appeared to be the center of a circle. When we met, the circle was stationed on Bank Street, but then he bought a loft on the southern edge of Soho where all these people reassembled.

For such a busy person, Emmanuel was the soul of calm—he spoke in a soft, gentle voice, often paused to reflect before speaking, as he held one of his little cheroots between his fingers, and his conversation was so even-tempered that no matter what was going on in his life that might be upsetting, he spoke of it with a reflective detachment. Yet he had made sure his life was anything but uneventful. How he had time to read at all perplexed me, yet read he did—he was reading everything by Julio Cortázar, for instance, when we met, and a disciple of Freud of whom I'd never heard. He also seemed to be going to virtually every movie that opened in New York, not to mention the newest restaurant, and the gym—yet, in the midst of this, maintaining the intellectual calm which I so enjoyed when we spoke. I think of him almost purely in terms of conversation; we seldom did things together; we mainly talked.

His wife, a good-looking woman with short blond hair, moved to the East Village to live with an American not long after her arrival in New York. Emmanuel's boyfriend was five or six years younger than he. Even when we met, Emmanuel began to complain about Jorge's behavior, character, and ethics, in a way I attributed to the tension that comes between two people who have been on a long trip together. But when an opportunity to visit Rio de Janeiro came up, and Emmanuel was not free to go, and Jorge and I went down together, he seemed the best of companions: cheerful, easygoing, uncomplaining. Nevertheless, on our return it became clear to me that Emmanuel wanted to get rid of him, so, when they did separate, Emmanuel purchased Jorge's interest in the loft—though the agreement specified that if Emmanuel should die before five years had passed, the loft would revert to Jorge.

Once Emmanuel was unattached, however, I learned this was a condition he did not like. He began spending hours cruising the piers on the Hudson; but he was inherently uxorial. That summer he shared a house with me and my friends at the beach. His friends dropped by: Patricio, the Argentine carpenter who resembled a quattrocento angel; Tony, the Spanish *loca*; Jean Michel, the publisher from Montreal; André, the French dealer in antiques with the beautiful Brazilian boyfriend. But Emmanuel, ever the anthropologist, the tourist, the foreigner, seemed to prize the much more ordinary Americans I introduced him to, simply because, in his eyes, I guess, they were natives, privy to the culture of Fire Island, the one in which he was now residing. He told me once that he had no type, that beauty did not matter to him.

The boyfriend who succeeded Jorge, I suppose, was not unattractive: a tall, skinny twenty-one-year-old from a family of nine kids on a farm in Illinois who had only one thing in common with Jorge—he was younger than Emmanuel—though Matthew was much younger. Matthew, the corn-fed youth from Illinois who had come east to study fashion, was a rather silly, shallow youth, I thought, but then we accept our friends' lovers and keep our mouths shut. There was something so American about his face it always reminded me of an ad for chewing gum: blue eyes, straight nose, dirty blond hair that he combed into a little pompadour. The little pompadour was hardly that of a rube, however; Matthew was enrolled in the Fashion Institute of Technology, worked the cosmetics counter at Bloomingdale's, and knew just about everything there was to know about fashion, cosmetics, and New York nightlife.

One always suspects a much younger boyfriend; one assumes the bond is purely sexual, that it will fade, and the young person disappear. Emmanuel and Matthew had met at the baths. He was one of those young people attracted to older men—there was a doctor in his past. He moved into Emmanuel's loft, and for the next few years they rented a house at the beach, danced at the Saint, took drugs, and went to the baths. Yet I was not surprised one day when Emmanuel told me he had no interest in the Saint, or the drugs they took, or the baths they went to afterward, except as a bond between him and Matthew. That was what mattered to Emmanuel. He was one of those people who cannot live without a partner. Emmanuel was happy with Matthew and that, for his friends, was all that mattered. As for Matthew: He was no intellectual, but he was smart, and it was fun to talk to someone in his generation. His style was not ours. Matthew wore red basketball sneakers and black 501s, big overcoats from used clothes stores in the East Village, the fifties pompadour, the clean-shaven face that fascinated because it was new and because it belonged to youth.

He was a bridge to another generation, the post-clone. Yet he evidently had little interest in his peers; he spent his time with Emmanuel and Emmanuel's friends, all in their thirties, forties, fifties. He sat there patiently on the big pillows, listening; then he went to the Saint and danced till ten A.M. He was not a big reader, and when he went to France with Emmanuel he could not understand the language. But he was ambitious. He was a hard worker. He went to school, and got a job at Bloomingdale's, and put in his hours behind the counter; and sometimes I looked at him in the loft with his older French lover, his summers on Fire Island, and thought: He is a lot further along than I was at that age—he was that ageless creature, someone who knew what he wanted.

Then one day, not long after he said they were looking for a third sexual partner, which indicated to me that their bond was fading in that regard, Emmanuel told me he'd gone to the doctor and learned his white blood cell count was abnormal, and that he felt tired. Thus began what seemed at the time simply Emmanuel's latest obsession. It was certainly a switch. Michel Foucault is said to have laughed on first hearing about AIDS—it was so obvious a fantasy of American puritanism—and Emmanuel too, at the start, told me he thought AIDS was one more example of the prudery of American culture. Now he was starting treatment for it. One hesitated, especially then, to ask about the details of a friend's health; one was afraid to hear he was not all right; things were depressing enough, the first years of the plague. So it was his friends who asked each other, "What does Emmanuel have? What exactly is wrong with him?" "He says he has

ARC, but I don't see any symptoms," someone said. He began going to a doctor uptown who advocated perfusions of vitamins into the blood (a new word, "perfusions"). He sat in an office on his lunch hour with other people whose arms were connected to machines that dripped vitamins into their veins as they read magazines. I pictured women under hair dryers in a Helen Hopkinson cartoon in the *New Yorker*, or a Ruth Draper monologue, or even Molière's Imaginary Invalid. He enrolled in an experimental drug program with a different doctor and kept the two physicians in the dark about each other so he could participate in both protocols, and on his lunch hour would rush from one to the other in a taxi, like a man in a Feydeau farce. All this I decided was simply part of Emmanuel's restless pursuit of the newest thing, in books, movies, places, health care. Emmanuel was always traveling, in other words; Matthew and the Saint, Fire Island and the perfusions, were just part of that. The only permanent thing was his restless curiosity—and the loft.

The fact that Emmanuel was now exposed (the euphemism for "infected") meant he could now return to the old pleasure of reading books. In the summer, on Fire Island, he would go to bed at a reasonable hour ("For a long time, I used to go to bed early," is the opening line of Proust) in order to preserve his health, or just stay in the city. Emmanuel no longer wanted to go out to the Pines with a boyfriend, take drugs, and dance, so he began staying home on weekends, while Matthew continued to go out. It was Matthew we saw at Tea Dance now. His presence there made me uneasy, however. There were many times when I wanted to tell Emmanuel that I was worried that Matthew was going to infect him, because Matthew was still going out to Fire Island and tricking, I assumed, when Emmanuel had stopped. Matthew, I feared, was the vector that made Emmanuel's caution meaningless—since what Matthew picked up would be brought home to the loft they shared. Who knows what really happened—when either man was infected?

That fall Emmanuel moved to Paris for three months to take a drug (HPA23) the Pasteur Institute was offering—the one for which Rock Hudson flew over in a state far worse than Emmanuel's, chartering his own 747, one of the famous images of the plague. Rock Hudson was visibly sick—kissing Linda Evans on the cover of the tabloid at the supermarket he looked like a vampire—but since we had still not seen any symptoms in Emmanuel, this made his friends wonder: Did Emmanuel know something the rest of us did not? Was he simply anticipating a future, forestalling a fate the rest of us would be mown down by because we were doing nothing? The Imaginary Invalid now became The Man on the Cutting Edge with the good sense to act before it was too late—even if Emmanuel wrote me that the doctors were having trouble cultivating the virus from his blood. Back in New York, Matthew enrolled at Hunter, and had a classmate move into the loft with him. Emmanuel wrote the long letters that only a recluse could write, about the books he was reading, the occasional need to move from one friend's apartment to another, the weather, his isolation. For three months he went out only to eat or to visit the clinic. He did not like Paris, he said, or the Parisians, and he concluded, during the course of the psychiatric therapy the clinic provided, and reading books written by a disciple of Freud who believed most illness was psychosomatic, that the reason he had AIDS was that he had a death wish.

Emmanuel completed the treatment, nevertheless, and then went to Southeast Asia, where Matthew joined him and Emmanuel's skepticism about AIDS increased. From a hotel on a beach in Thailand he wrote that AIDS was like Vietnam: a creation of the press—a hysteria, a frame of mind, induced by our exposure to the media—and that, on this beach, favored by hippies, far from the United States, it seemed very distant. But they were not going to stay there long. "Matthew is not a good traveler," Emmanuel wrote, "he does not like being so far away from hamburgers and Fire Island, I believe he finds this all a bit déclassé, and of course it is true—Thailand, or Bangkok, at least, is just the brothel of Europe." In Thailand they decided not to have sex with each other—or rather Matthew indicated his preference that they not—and so the sex which they'd been forced to modify since Emmanuel's blood test, a sex with precautions, now vanished completely; and I wondered how long the rest would last. Not very long. That summer—back on Fire Island—they announced a breakup.

That still left the summer to get through in the beach house, and there was also the loft in the city. There were in short all the problems that come from any separation; and to make it worse—it made everything worse—there was the disease. A friend who saw Matthew at Tea Dance that summer said he was looking so thin, almost anorexic, that Bloomingdale's had asked him to quit. (A cadaverous figure out of Edvard Munch is not what sells perfume.) Emmanuel, however, looked fine. Indeed, he did look healthy when I saw him that fall on a visit to Manhattan; though he'd told me, when I called from a pay phone on the corner, that he would come down, instead of the usual "Come up!" When he reached the sidewalk, he said that Matthew was home sick. Matthew was now sicker than he was, Emmanuel explained, and he could not stay out very long. He only had time for breakfast. Matthew had been in the hospital, but was now taking his medications at home. His mother—a retired registered nurse—had arrived to help care for him. The three of them—Matthew, his mother, Emmanuel—were all sleeping in the same big bed. Emmanuel himself had contracted pneumonia a few months ago but had responded so favorably to the medicine he had not even been hospitalized, though he did have Kaposi's sarcoma.

We had breakfast in a restaurant on the border between Soho and Tribeca—a bright room with handsome waiters—beside a table covered with pies and cakes, the glint of silver, water glasses, mirrors, chrome, the plates of waffles smothered in cream and apples, the busy, bright, expensive air of a Sunday brunch in New York around us. Later, when we had finished grocery shopping and walked back to the loft, he turned and asked me if I'd ask a friend of ours Matthew very much liked to visit. The friend and I went the next day. Matthew came out, nicely dressed, on his feet, and entertained us. ("Ah, he is much better when you are here!" said Emmanuel.) We talked of Fire Island, summer, fashion. I asked where to find good khaki pants. Then he pulled up his blouse to show us the permanent IV that had been surgically implanted in his chest: a plastic plate below his collarbone to which the tubes were attached. He hooked himself up. The nurse came twice a week. His mother—a gray-haired, bespectacled woman with a gentle voice—went into the kitchen to clean up, and, when she had finished that, came out and began to Windex some of the windows at the end of the loft. "How dirty they get," she said when I passed her on my way out—as if that were the only grime that had accumulated in Manhattan, I thought.

"He was wonderful," I said to my friend on the street.

"Very wonderful," he said. Then he shuddered. "I didn't like seeing that thing, though."

"I thought he looked wonderful, too," I said.

"I thought he looked awful," said my friend.

"I don't know what I'm doing here," Emmanuel said when we took a walk to the Hudson River down the same street the next day, and crossed to the Esplanade, busy with cars, bicycles, and boats offshore. "I feel I am just maintaining myself, just trying not to die. It's very strange." He said this in the same calm voice he used for everything: dispassionate, detached. I did not ask if he resented having to care for Matthew, after trying to get him to leave; or if it frightened him to see in Matthew the progress of an illness he had; or if he ever thought the evenings at the Saint, the baths, the drugs he had taken because they amused Matthew, were what had caused all of this. There was no point. They were stuck together now; something unforeseen had imprisoned them in that loft, just two of many tragedies being played out in rooms all over the city, scenes that would never make the newspaper, or even the gossip of the dinner table, because they were exactly what everyone wanted hidden behind walls. Pain, Hannah Arendt wrote, is the last private thing.

A few months later Matthew decided he'd had enough of pain, of tubes, medications, and vomiting. One Saturday he announced his decision to refuse the fluids that were keeping him alive. He called his doctor. The doctor did not disagree. So on a Saturday afternoon, one of those Saturdays when Matthew used to stand behind the counter at Bloomingdale's helping women select the correct face powder and blush, he opted out—and by the following morning, around six A.M., on a day when, years before, he and Emmanuel had been dancing to what was called Sleaze Music at the Saint (the best music, the music you wait all night for, the music that comes only at the end of an evening, that is finally relaxed, sensual, melancholy, the cream of the night), he died.

"He never complained," Emmanuel wrote. "He did it all, and his mother, too, with dignity. During the night he said a few things—It's dark, I'm scared, Hold my hand!—but that was all. In the early morning, he died, and we called the police. The police came. Then the undertaker—from Soho—a woman in Norma Kamali—put him in a bag. Very chic. His mother left yesterday after his cremation and when I walked her to the cab, she said to me: 'I think the reason I was put on earth was for these last two months.'"

By this time Emmanuel was himself sick. After ringing the bell and climbing the stairs, I would see him open the door with his little sing-song of welcome (*"Bon jour"*), take off my shoes, and follow him into the kitchen for the chicken or steak he usually prepared. Emmanuel was so well mannered, so uncomplaining, that after he'd served you dinner at a little table, and we'd retired to the big overstuffed sofa in the main section of the loft, he would pull over the dolly on which his IV medicine hung in plastic bags, insert the needle into the indwelling catheter, and we'd go right on talking about books, mutual friends, with perfect equanimity, like the guests at the end of *Quo Vadis* who go on conversing while Petronius bleeds to death. He was also very funny. One day as we sat there talking, with Emmanuel connected to his IV drip, I said that gay men seemed to think that at least oral sex was safe, and he said, "Then you can suck me." That put the issue in a way that brought me up short. Each time I visited Emmanuel I did so with my breath held—excited to see him, admiring his aplomb, fearful and horrified. Afterward, the moment I was on the street, I felt equal parts admiration and depression.

When Matthew died Emmanuel was seeing a therapist; and— at either the therapist's suggestion, or his own inspiration—he began to write a book. (When the writer Robert Ferro first revealed his illness, my first reaction was: "You must keep a journal!" But this suggestion, like the idea that facing death will produce great art, ignored the fact that writers cannot, really, choose their subjects. Robert ended up not keeping a journal at all; he wrote a novel instead; it was Emmanuel who kept a record.) I was sure he would tell the story of Matthew's death in it. But true to that reserve, that sense of dignity, that tone of ironic calm with which Emmanuel's book, *Mortal Embrace*, is imbued, he did not. He changed their names, though the mother had since died, and dealt with what could have formed the libretto of a three-act opera in a few phrases. But the experience of Matthew's illness and death, he admits in his book, changed him forever; and gave him the courage, or inspiration, to go on himself.

This project was only one of the things that made visiting Emmanuel, alone in the loft now, unlike visiting anyone else I knew with AIDS: the manuscript's acceptance by an editor at Farrar Straus, praise for it from Susan Sontag and Richard Howard, publication in France, a trip back to Paris to appear on the TV show *Apostrophes.* The appearance on *Apostrophes* made Emmanuel's struggle with AIDS almost glamorous. Yet the assumption he speaks of at the outset of *Mortal Embrace*—that all people with AIDS will die, the assumption that everyone around the person with AIDS has—was also mine.

Still, now that his fifteen minutes of fame had arrived, Emmanuel had become one of those people granted the Faustian bargain: The thing that was giving him success was the same thing that was killing him. "Living with AIDS" is the subtitle of the book—and that's exactly what he was doing. His nurse, he said, was a macabre man who came once a week to change medicines (and tells the narrator of *Mortal Embrace* about how poorly his other patients are doing). Emmanuel told me about running into a well-known man on the AIDS fund-raising circuit one day in a doctor's waiting room. He wondered about the competence or incompetence of an editor. All this, as Emmanuel's book came to be, made dinners with him fun. The wit remained. The day the *Times* ran an article by another writer with a book out about AIDS, he put the paper down, turned to me and said, "But I have more lesions than he does."

His book spoke of emotions no one else had admitted to: his anger at people who were still healthy, his fear that Matthew's illness had sapped his own strength, his guilt after Matthew allowed himself to die that Matthew had done so for him, his feeling that AIDS had rescued him from the "mediocrity and materialism" of his previous life.

But when the sun went down, and he put on Strauss's "Four Last Songs," and we retired to the sofa in that big room where once the Brazilians and Argentines had played, and Matthew had died, it was hard not to escape the image Emmanuel summoned up at the end of *Mortal Embrace*: Hitler's bunker.

Emmanuel's loft was on the southernmost corner of Soho, on the fifth floor of a building one approached across a narrow street lined with an apartment building that an artist had painted a beautiful turquoise, a basketball court and playground, an empty, weed-grown lot, and, beyond them, the spires of lower Manhattan over which the moon would rise. Its long row of windows looked out on a beautiful skyline. But all I could think of when I looked back from the street was how its occupants had been reduced to one. Now his only company was his book.

It was some company: the praise from Sontag, the appearance on *Apostrophes*, the letter from Roger Straus expressing his sense of honor at publishing it. All these were the things a writer dreams of, and they were coming true for Emmanuel; so that when the book finally did appear, and I opened up the *New York Times Book Review* one Sunday, and found, along with Paul Monette, Emmanuel himself staring out at me, there was something anticlimactic about it all—especially when the review sounded a note that was in almost all the American reviews of *Mortal Embrace*: Emmanuel had overdone the military metaphor. When I protested that this did not matter, Emmanuel replied, calmly and sweetly, "But it means my book is a failure."

Perhaps—but it was still a very handsome book I found in stacks in a store on the Upper West Side my last visit to New York, when no one answered Emmanuel's phone, and I did not even see him. After I left New York I got news of Emmanuel through others. My last letter to him he did not answer. Then one day Jorge called and said that Emmanuel was in a coma in St. Luke's. The virus had reached his brain. His father and stepmother and sister had come from France. He came out of the coma, he was sent home, and there, in that loft, his stepmother took him in her arms, and sang him a lullaby as he died. At the end of *Mortal Embrace*, Emmanuel said that his real home was not the loft, or New York, but the French language. Still, I could not help but think: His Romance with America had killed him.

Tuesday Nights

TUESDAY NIGHTS WE meet in a Quaker meetinghouse on a quiet residential street in Gainesville—a city in north-central Florida—just two blocks from the campus of the university. The discussion group is several years old. "It started out at The Drugstore," says a friend who has gone to it intermittently since the beginning, "and it was *won*derful. Kids would come in and say, 'I think I'm gay, but I'm not sure.' People would *weep*. It was so moving, and wide open. But then everything was in those days," this nostalgic hippie sighs. "Then it was taken over by an assistant professor who used it as a *trick farm* [the sixties becoming the seventies] until one night he found himself speaking to an empty room [the seventies becoming the eighties]. He had slept with everyone, you see. So it lay fallow for a while, and now it's in its third phase. More sober and level-headed, but without those *won*derful moments of revelation." Indeed there is something middle-aged about the group run by a doctor who, amazingly, comes up each week with a new speaker, topic, or film. The core group of faithful attendants comprises a psychiatrist, a schoolteacher, a writer, a librarian, a retailer, an attorney, and only occasionally—in the fall, when students come back to school—the freshmen who spill their souls (as in the old days) in a frenzy of coming out, and then never appear again. Where they go I do not know. The once-competing organization of gay and lesbian students at the university is now defunct; a charismatic leader, since graduated, has not been replaced by anyone, and a quarrel over funds with the student government has left its speaker's program in disarray.

There are always a few wild cards, too, on Tuesday nights, and that is part of the reason one goes: to see the person you've never seen before, or the ones who come every three months or so; the recently arrived student or assistant professor who knows no one in town yet and brings with him a burst of northern energy from Ann Arbor or Berkeley, and then vanishes again. But mainly one finds The Group—of ten or twelve men who come every week and even dine together in a different restaurant each Thursday, and who constitute what a golf foursome or poker club must have for my father: a dependable bunch of men with whom one can relax, unwind, and talk on a weekly basis. For what I prize most about this evening, perhaps, as I sit beside a whirring fan in summer, or a space heater on cold nights, is what characterizes this particularly leafy street, this plain wooden house: a certain camaraderie and calm.

The house is shared—someone said—by a fugitive family from Central America, but I have no way of knowing if this is so, since we are the only ones in it on Tuesday nights. But this rumor emphasizes the marginal, sub rosa nature of our shared identity . . . even within the homosexual population itself. There must be three to five thousand gay men in Gainesville, but here at the meeting there are only twenty or so. I have friends in this town who wouldn't be caught dead here on Tuesday nights. Ten years ago I would never have come to a meeting of this sort. People who belonged to groups like this, or went to the gay churches, were, I assumed, people who did not have the nerve to look for a partner in the actual world: the baths, beaches, and bars. In the old days tricking was the way we met people. But things are reversed now. The idea of tricking seems absurd. The mating dance has slowed down considerably. Everyone here hopes he will meet someone, I suppose—though most of them are attached already; perhaps only when the problem of sex has been solved does one have time or energy to spare for its sublimations. But that does not explain Gaytalk entirely. To meet somebody may be the reason I went to my first meeting—a reason reflected in the behavior of lesbians who come once, find no other women, and do not return—because the bars in Gainesville are cliquish (friends talking to each other, while the hapless stranger swims around like a penguin among ice floes that are already occupied). But the second time I came—after giving up, and going back to the bars for a year—I was having an AIDS anxiety attack.

That night, by coincidence, a male nurse from Ocala was giving a talk on this subject, and having fears aired in this manner helped, the way calling the Gay Switchboard—though you use it only once or twice in your life—in a strange city helps. The third time I went back, it was a blend of these two motives: fear and longing. Fear and longing seem to cancel each other out these days. Fear and longing are, furthermore, played out differently in a town this size, which doesn't provide the vacuum of anonymity a city like New York does—a vacuum through which sparks fly so easily—because the man you go home with will almost surely be in the bar the next night. But fear and longing persist, and this place seems the perfect compromise. Here the plague seems a bit removed, as I listen to a lecture on Michelangelo on this plain wooden folding chair as the fan whirs and I watch a student come back to the boardinghouse next door, his blond head passing under the porch light. I feel, in fact, as if I'm in church.

From the first time I went, I have considered this a sort of prayer meeting, in fact. The gathering together, the communion (of minds), the calm, the straw basket that is passed afterward to obtain donations, all remind me of church. No one stands up to confess deep dark secrets, or testifies, but there is, on our folding chairs, beside the fake pine-paneled walls, under a bulb in the ceiling, the atmosphere of an evening service in some country church. Here for an hour passion is transcended, if that is not too fancy a way of putting it. Here for a moment we enjoy what a friend in New York (who greets with joy an inclination to go to the movies instead of the baths) would call "a neutral activity." Here we do something that does not center around cruising. That, for gay men, is church. Gay men, of course, went to church as much as other children, but when they grew up, found themselves outside the church and the culture they were otherwise part of. Hence Dignity, the gay synagogue, AA, psychiatrists, gay books, and Gaytalk on Tuesday nights. Times have changed, and changed radically, but each one of us is still trying to find the same old things: sex, and love, and self-respect.

Sex, love, and self-respect are hard enough to balance in life, period, without having to do it as a person whose biological identity seems at variance with his sexual one. How to integrate our homosexuality with the rest of our selves, our lives—our family, our society, our upbringing—was a problem a minority, not a majority, of the gay men I knew were able to solve before the plague. Most of us just kept everything in compartments. Most of us led double, triple, quadruple lives, changing costumes as actors do, masking our intelligence, emphasizing our bodies, feeling our fate depended on the shape of our mustache, the size of our dick. But you can juggle the apples of discord only so long. When desire begins to burn off, like morning haze, it leaves the rest of our personalities more visible. "I've read all of Proust and Henry James, I just got a promotion at the bank to systems manager," a friend wrote me in 1977. "So what am I doing at four A.M. in Sheridan Square, hailing a cab with shit on my dick?" *Having the time of your life,* I would have answered had we both been twenty-one. But we were not, and that was part of the problem: What youth and lust camouflage, age and abstinence bring into relief—the contradictions of being gay. The plague has only increased the vividness of the questions in those who've survived thus far. It has made dangerous the sex that was used to answer all doubts, cater to all moods, avoid all problems. "I belong to a GMHC Safe Sex Study Group," the friend who had his moment of truth at four A.M. in Sheridan Square in 1977 writes me this week. "Everyone is either a little or very crazy, and all ask the same question: If every gay man in the Rancid Apple is terrified of getting AIDS, why can't these dizzy clones settle down and play house with one another?"

It's one of the questions I think about as I sit in the Quaker meetinghouse, miles from the epicenter, but still part of the plague. ("The virus is here, in the community," says one of the doctors. Just recently, three men died of AIDS in Gainesville in one week.) When the plague began, I thought homosexual society would wither away—if men could not sleep with one another, why would they go out to baths, bars, or beaches? I was wrong. There is still some need to be together—even to hear someone deliver a book report on Kaplan's biography of Walt Whitman, or a history of the Mattachine Society. The topics vary in importance, no doubt, to each individual. A graduate student describes a study of early childhoods of people who later became homosexual. The next week a lawyer explains the mechanics of making wills in which a homosexual partner is the beneficiary. A psychiatrist surveys the APA's definition of homosexuality over the years. A man reviews local political candidates (pointing out that a public endorsement by our group may in fact harm, rather than help, the candidate we prefer). The pastor of the local gay church speaks, followed by a woman from a local department store who lectures on cosmetics. A teacher discusses the various charitable drives (Toys for Tots, Food for the Indigent on Thanksgiving) the group might participate in. A doctor brings in his favorite opera records. Another doctor, his favorite wines. In its improvised, eclectic course, the group moves forward like some snail, incorporating whatever enters its path, feeding on its members' expertise, which is more fun, I think, than something more strictly political. That would be too narrow. Homosexuality is more than politics; and more than sex; and under the ceiling bulb, while the students float by on bicycles outside on green summer evenings, this quiet room seems very much like Life. Moments of exquisite boredom (the classroom clichés of the visiting psychologist) are followed by breathless revelation—the student who lists his reasons for not telling his parents he's gay, and then tells us what his fraternity brothers said when he told them. These are the stories I love to hear. At the end of each meeting, we are asked to go around the room and introduce ourselves. Then the straw basket is passed from person to person, the speaker is thanked and applauded, and we stand up and talk to friends. When I first came here, I had none and fled to my car in a paroxysm of shyness—something newcomers still do—but now I linger with the rest on the sidewalk outside, like any congregation.

The modest, unstated proposition that Gaytalk rests upon is this: that the rational (Come, let us reason together) can bring into focus what is irrational (Eat my big dick, you worm). "I was a problem," said Oscar Wilde, "for which there was no solution." But sitting here listening to men of different ages, circumstances, talk about their version of the problem, one feels that if there is not—to the problem of Life, either—it is pleasing nonetheless to assume we can reach one. Hearing them argue is an opportunity to stand back from the bewildering contradictions of being gay—to put things in perspective, to talk, as reasonably as possible, about things that may not be reasonable at all in real life. When we leave the Quaker meetinghouse, I feel a magic circle has been broken. For beyond the screen door is the real world, with its separate compartments, its balancing act.

In fact most of us get in our cars after the discussion, drive straight to the bar, and regroup inside its very different environment, talking to one another as our eyes roam the room, checking out the patrons who did not come to Gaytalk. (The modest, unstated proposition the bar rests on is: Everything can still be solved with a lover.) Would Gaytalk be pointless without the Ambush afterward? Would it be possible if once every six weeks I couldn't drive to the Club Baths in Jacksonville—where men meet, but do not discuss much? (There's a Gaytalk that takes place in steamrooms.) I don't know. It's useless to pretend that sex is *not* at the center of homosexual life—the reason these men want to be with one another—and yet at this point in time it (sex) seems less central than it used to be. Hence, Gaytalk. The last slide of David—the ideal—fades from the screen, and the speaker asks, "Are there any questions?" Lots, but no doubt they can't be answered. One must still make the connection on one's own between Michelangelo and what waits outside, the minute one opens that screen door—the screen door past which young men ride on their bicycles, oblivious of the problems in which they play the central role, immured in youth and beauty.

Trust

WE WERE SITTING on a porch in Florida this afternoon leafing through the portfolio of photographs a friend had brought over, half watching the butterflies in the geraniums, when I came to the portrait of a handsome man and asked who this was. A man in San Francisco, my friend replied, who had just walked out on his lover. "And you know what his exit line was?" he said. "'When you get the night sweats, you'll know you've got it.'"

"What do you mean?" I said.

"He has AIDS," my friend said of the good-looking man with the mustache and wavy hair. "He had it when he began the relationship, but he told his lover if they kept a positive attitude, they wouldn't get it. Now, of course, the boyfriend's got it, and when it happened," he said, pointing to the photograph, "he packed his bags and walked out, saying, 'When you get the night sweats, you'll know you've got it.'"

"But—but—," I said, incredulous, dumbfounded, staring at this handsome man in the photograph, "who is he?"

"He's smart," said my friend. "He's a psychologist. He wanted to get AIDS."

"Wanted to?" I said.

"He went out to the baths, just when it began, when he knew it was dangerous, and put his ass up in the air," he said. "He wanted to get it."

"But how does the lover feel?" I said, pointing to the adjacent photograph, a man with a dark beard and friendly eyes. "The one he gave it to?"

"He has chronic hepatitis," my friend said. "His stomach is swelled out to here," he said, drawing a potbelly in the air. "He just thinks it's one more version of being dumped on by life."

When I first heard stories—like this one—I didn't believe them; they belonged to that realm of rumor in which the gossip is made up out of whole cloth, merely because it's so dramatic. No one would do that in real life, I thought. It just isn't believable. The first story I heard—about five years ago—involved the death of a decorator in New York whose brother flew east from California to attend the wake and stayed with a man I'll call Bob. The brother was attractive, and one evening after the wake, talking things over before the fireplace, Bob and the brother ended up having sex. When the sex was over, Bob asked the brother what he would do with all the money he'd inherit from the decorator; the brother replied, "Spend it. I have AIDS, too."

Surely this was made up, I thought; no one could possibly do that. It's certainly true, as Scott Fitzgerald wrote, that a sense of the fundamental decencies is parceled out unequally at birth, but I could not even imagine the person who would knowingly expose another person to the virus. I had trouble with people who littered; I wanted them arrested and given the electric chair. I knew the junk that clogged the mangroves in which gay men cruised at Virginia Key in Miami, soiled the dunes at the gay beach south of Jacksonville, was proof that gay people, yes, *even gay people,* were slobs. But I had perhaps a rather exalted vision of homosexuals; I suspected, in some chamber of my heart, that they were, well, neater, nicer, more sensitive than the rest. Mayor Lindsay used to say, "The trouble with New York is that there are too many slobs." But I didn't include the gay community in that; I found it hard to believe—and very discouraging—that they even littered.

But then a few years of the plague, and more stories of this sort, passed, and the next one I heard about someone I knew sounded a little more imaginable: A young man just out of the hospital after a bout of pneumocystic pneumonia went to the Saint to celebrate, met someone, and took him home. Hmmmm. One *would* go to the Saint to celebrate, perhaps, that was not unlikely, and perhaps in the mood created by the place, the dancing, one might meet someone, and . . . but there it stopped. People do not murder other people casually. Surely he would have told the person he had just got out of the hospital, and so on.

And then, shortly after hearing this story, I read about Fabian Bridges. Fabian Bridges was just a newspaper article at first— about a male prostitute shunted back and forth between two cities that didn't want him, because he had AIDS and the judge thought the only solution was to put him on a bus out of town. Put this way, I felt sorry for Fabian Bridges; then I saw him in a documentary on television. On television Fabian Bridges was seen haunting the seedier parts of cities (those blocks that look exactly alike in Pittsburgh, Houston, Jacksonville, New York: the dirty bookstores, the theaters, the parking lots), after being asked by a doctor in the most patient, cajoling, restrained manner, to stop having sex. Stop having sex was what Fabian somehow seemed unable to do—though he voiced a mild regret at having ejaculated inside a customer (a man he'd come to like). This wistful regret was the only one Fabian Bridges evinced; friends who saw the film explained him away with brain infection—the virus had already destroyed his ability to act morally. But I wasn't so sure; it seemed possible to me Fabian Bridges was just one of those horrors—a morally inert succubus drifting through life without much will to do right or wrong. Who knows? The gay community in Texas did what the courts and police could not—took Fabian in, got him off the street—and then death took him off the planet. But not before, one assumes, he had taken others with him.

We read daily now of prostitutes of both sexes who refuse to stop working, even though they have AIDS. There is an ex-American army sergeant being tried in Germany right now for having had sex with three men and not telling them he had the virus; the case has been clouded by the fact that one of them, a Spaniard, also had AIDS at the time. My, my. It just goes on and on. Admit the principle, and there is no end to the permutations.

I was watching TV with a friend the evening the death of Rock Hudson was announced. After asking me in a curious voice why gay men were so promiscuous, my friend then inquired, "Why did you *trust* one another?" The question gave me a moment's pause; I had never thought of it in those terms before—terms of trust. I said, "Because there was no reason not to. Everything could be cured with some form of penicillin." Yet now that I reflect on it all, it seems to me that not antibiotics but trust was the thing that made that life possible: the assumption that the person you slept with would not knowingly infect you with anything vile. Trust was the basis of the whole system—the Visa card that sent you to Brazil, Berlin, or California with the prospect of romance. (The thing that impelled people to go these places, soon after the plague appeared in New York, in fact, on the assumption that It hadn't arrived there yet.) There were exceptions to all this, of course. I got crabs in those days more times than I could count; by the twentieth time, I was less strict about waiting a few days after dousing myself with A-200 before going out again. I got amoebas and learned, after the fact, I'd been exposed to hepatitis; but I considered most of these just occupational hazards, germs swimming in the community pool, and not the malicious, much less lethal, act of any particular person. True, there were nights when, at the baths, I would see a man leave someone's room and the door to that room open a moment later to take on a new visitor—and I would think, *The fat, lazy cow. Can't even go downstairs and shower between encounters.* And in my disgust I would eventually walk past that open door to see who the slob was. He was always someone ordinary, I mean, without any distinguishing marks that set him apart from everyone else at the baths; and that, of course, is the trouble with trust now.

The rumor that AIDS had been spread by an airline steward had been around several years; the version I heard featured an Australian on Air Qantas. The airline steward, of course, has always personified a certain aspect of gay life—the most complete version of the fantasy; to be a new face in Rome, Paris, Cairo, London, Madrid—all in the same week, to sleep not with everyone in your gym, but with the whole world. It seemed, at a certain age, the only thing to do; an adventure one would be a fool not to spend at least a year on. Promiscuity and jet travel were somehow twins—synergistic. How else to get It from a green monkey in the interior of Africa to a penthouse in New York? The tracing of Patient Zero in Randy Shilts's new book on AIDS is not only a dramatic case of mystery solving; it's the culmination of all those stories about this person—this gay person in whom I could not quite believe—that have been floating around for years now. No wonder the mainstream press picked up on it. It finally gives a face to what has been so far faceless. It crystallizes all the anger and moral outrage that have been gathering without an object. The steward from Air Canada reduces a force, a vast dilemma, to what even an age accustomed to institutional power hungers for—the story of a single human being making a choice between right and wrong, good and evil. Gaetan Dugas, apparently, made the wrong choice. Gaetan personifies, in what we've read of him so far, a recognizable type in gay life: the vain and careless Queen. The Pretty Boy with the not-so-pretty value system. The Moral Slob. The Femme, oh very, Fatale. Flying from place to place, the man at the baths who—I presume—opened his door a moment after the last man had left and did not bother to go downstairs to shower; who, when the lights came up, if what we read is true, commented casually on his Kaposi's sarcoma as "the new gay cancer. Perhaps you'll get it, too."

A friend with AIDS gave some advice about having sex nowadays that still seems excellent: "Have sex," he said, "as if everyone is infected." What better guide? Standing in the Jewel in New York, watching the men go up and down the aisle, I can easily imagine now that some have AIDS. (In fact, someone told me last week that people with AIDS go there.) Why not? What else would you do if you had AIDS? Would you not more than ever have to be there, to cruise, to forget, to feel alive? Fabian Bridges, Patient Zero, are only extreme versions of something in many of us; we have all fudged reality a bit in the past five years, I suspect— behaved with standards that now seem to us lax and self-deluded. Indeed, the longer the plague goes on, and the more pervasive our exposure to it, the more unappetizing sex becomes—sex that seems risky, that is. But this psychological barrier, this distaste, was not always there; it took years to coalesce and solidify. The trouble is we know now that a person can give someone AIDS in several moral states—not knowing he has it, knowing he has it but not thinking what he does is dangerous ("Just keep a positive attitude!"), knowing he has it and passing it on out of despair, revenge, indifference, hatred, selfishness, or sheer amorality; having a hole where the conscience should be, or a vengeful feeling that what the community gave to him, he can give back. It's the same principle, after all—the man who goes out with crabs and the man who goes out with AIDS. Only crabs can be killed with A-200; the virus cannot. And with that fact, all trust dissolves.

The truth is, most people are not amoral—most of them care very much about not endangering someone they have sex with—but the fact that some are is enough to shut down the whole system. It's a bit like the Tylenol scare—most of the bottles on the shelf were surely safe, but the possibility that one of them might contain poison was enough to make the manufacturer withdraw the product. AIDS destroys trust. We cannot possibly investigate, much less be responsible for, what the man we are attracted to has done with the past five or seven years of his life. We can't guarantee ourselves. This limits sex with each passing year. It shuts down a whole system of behavior, a community; it builds a wall between each of us. AIDS is a form of pollution; in this case, polluted semen and blood. We've spoiled even that. AIDS is a form of terrorism—sex becomes Paris the summer the bombs went off. Nobody goes. Like Central Park—empty at night because everyone's afraid of muggers—homosexual life becomes a vast empty space from which everyone has withdrawn. We look at one another not merely as appetizing possibilities, possible boyfriends, fantasies, pleasure—we look at each other as lethal instruments, threats, dangers, obstacle courses, things one would have to sift through a whole host of tests in order to eat. Sodomy—the central ritual from which all else proceeded—is out of the question. Kissing, fellatio, all must be weighed. The tree of sex shrivels up. When I go to the Jewel in New York, or the baths in Jacksonville, I see what I've come to call the Same Nine People. They're not exactly nine, and they're not always the same, but almost, and you get the point. The fact is, there do not have to be a lot of Patient Zeros out there to destroy the way of life we had evolved; there just has to be one. As long as a friend writes me from San Diego that a man he knows in an AZT program out there called to ask him if he had any ethyl chloride for the march in Washington—because he thought it the greatest cruising opportunity ever—well, that's enough.

One afternoon last spring we took a walk down to the Morton Street pier and found a wire-mesh fence along its perimeter to keep people away from the rotting timbers at the edge. Not in New York, of course: There were still people sunbathing along the margin, beyond the concrete divider and the silver fence. One in particular was nude; the sun gleamed on every pore of his bare back and buttocks, the tiny hairs on his forearm and neck—and I stood there for a moment staring at him, wondering which one of us was confined. The nude beyond the chicken wire fence was one of those images that express the whole dilemma. Or the nude behind the Plexiglas panel, in the bookstore off Times Square a friend of mine repairs to after an exhausting day at work—the individual booths are all separated by transparent walls, like a handball court one can see into, and the men stand in their separate cells, jerking off to one another. Or the dance floor at Track's. It's filled with people dancing; the handsome men take their shirts off at a certain point, as they used to formerly, observing rituals practiced by a court that no longer exists. It is all muted, a ghost of itself, all difficult to explain, till I see a muscular man beating a stick against a gourd while a woman dances to his syncopation and, as she whirls around, read what the sweatshirt she's wearing says: CHOOSE LIFE. That is the caption that explains the dance now, and our whole community. You've heard of postmodern. This is post-trust.

The Way
We Live Now

"T HERE'S SOMETHING DIFFERENT about gay New York," a friend writes from Manhattan this May, "but I can't figure it out. For instance, I've noticed that nobody talks about AIDS anymore. As recently as a year ago, it was the topic; three years ago, it was the only topic. My friend who does ministry to PWAs says it's just a massive dose of denial and a desire to live even with dark clouds hanging over us and to carry on."

Strangely enough, I've had the same feeling for a while—that AIDS is no longer the topic it used to be in the media, either; either because there are no news developments to report, or because, in journalism, as in every other field, everything is critical for just fifteen minutes. AIDS already seems like last season's story. Which means I've the feeling we are in a lull—one of those deceptive pauses in the action that beguiles us into thinking that this is the way life's going to be now, for the indefinite future— but which, in reality, never lasts. Lulls, in fact, make me nervous.

They always precede disaster. But that's how it seems now as I write this in late May 1989, the last summer of a surreal decade.

The weather, as I sit here on the porch in Florida, has changed several times in the past hour. Clouds form on the other side of the lake; the sky turns gray, and I watch a wall of rain move over the lake, drench the yard, and move on; then the sun comes out, it's hot and steamy and I can smell the grass. Twenty minutes later, the sun vanishes behind another mass of clouds; the yard darkens; the lake turns silver. More rain. And then more sun. It will probably go on like this all day, and for the next few months. It's what this lull is like—a patchwork of constantly changing conditions making up what one calls with a single word, weather.

Another friend writes this week from San Francisco, where he and his lover have just tested Positive for antibodies to the virus, about why they don't talk about AIDS: "Bob and I are pretty much totally *over* at this point. I cannot tolerate his negativity concerning his Positive status. He *refuses* to be hopeful or do any-thing to attempt to deal with this entire nightmare—which— yes, it is—but lots of other guys are dealing with this, also—and their lives are progressing. Bob's is *not*—at this time. He has quit his job and gone on Disability and is living off the interest from his trust—his life is hardly even *life*—he sleeps all the time and just lies around and reads. He obviously needs help—but God forbid I should remind him of that—so I have given up—as I do not want stress and conflict in my life right now—only joy and hope and *good* thoughts." So he's going out that evening, he says, to a party being given for men who have tested Positive, to meet someone who will give him the support he needs.

And that's how it is, the Wednesday before the weekend that not only begins the summer, but seems to be a gay holiday in the way few other of our official holidays are: Memorial Day. The present silence does not mean in any way that AIDS has gone away. Even my impression that the media had dropped the subject was changed, for instance, when *20/20* ran a story last night about a young Jewish woman, the only child of a Park Avenue family, who contracted AIDS, she thinks, by sleeping one time with a bisexual bartender from Studio 54 six years ago. The segment is moving—especially the family's decision to go public with the facts, and her decision to tour college campuses to warn other people her age: It can happen. The new twist, I guess, that induced *20/20* to feature what has, in a sense, ceased to be news must be AIDS among college kids.

The Jacksonville newspaper the same day carries a story announcing that the United States has lifted its ban on visitors to this country who've tested Positive, after protests that a Dutch man was refused entry in Minneapolis. Meanwhile, the *Village Voice* wants to know if Compound Q is the cure; and the argument continues among activists and journalists whether or not HIV is the cause. Panels are held. People argue. But these elements have all been part of the mix for some time now.

So is the variety of reactions to the situation among the friends I am in touch with. One says he's living on his publisher's advance for books because he doesn't even know if he'll ever hand them in, since, "Everyone's going to be dead in two years anyway." Another has just moved to Seattle to begin a new life. A friend in New York says he has not had sex in six years. Another who has just moved to Key West is having so much sex there he suggests that SILENCE = DEATH is not the only logo that should be on T-shirts; NO SEX = DEATH is another.

Another friend—a bartender from San Diego—is going to New York for Memorial Day weekend. I tell him to make sure he goes out to Fire Island, give him some friends' phone numbers, and then think: In the old days, a handsome Californian would be a present, but now, the meaning of a handsome Californian is entirely changed.

But when I say this to a friend in New York on the phone, he scoffs, "AIDS is now something you refer to in part of a conversation about other things. People have completely adapted to it, and are living around it."

That must be why my correspondent says nobody talks about it in New York anymore. One cannot expect people to live in a state of perpetual horror and outrage. Eventually they subside. Fatigue sets in, burnout, boredom, acceptance—and the attention span turns to something else. How could it be otherwise? Yet all of this is strange. That is, what's new about AIDS now is the fact that nothing *is* new. This package of facts is *it*—this mixture of health and sickness, fear and accommodation, action and inertia, participation and withdrawal. It's all settled down into a pattern, and become—along with AZT and pentamidine, the HIV test, the division of people into Positive and Negative—a way of life. A way of life described tellingly in an article by Victor F. Zonana called "Survivor's Syndrome: AIDS Takes Toll on Ones Left Behind" in the May 6 *Los Angeles Times*. This odd sense of malaise isn't just my imagination. This article, which one wishes had been written long before this, is doubly fascinating because it *has* appeared now—the eighth year into the plague—as if the dust has settled, things have fallen back to earth, and we can actually speak of survivors. With one exception, apparently: the people who've survived.

"Have you ever wondered why you have been spared?" a seventy-year-old married man from Seattle I have been corresponding with for five years wrote recently. "I know the question is very personal, which may be why you didn't want to answer it in your last letter." I wrote back, "I did not mean to evade your question about surviving. The answer is simple: No one who has survived thinks he has survived. That is, most gay men who've lost friends have no explanation, do not think this thing is over, still don't know what's going on, and are superstitious enough to believe that the moment they think they're a survivor, they'll get sick. Because, you see, the time lag—the latency period—is so very long." Odd, isn't it? One of the most striking things about the tumult of the past eight years (and the new modus vivendi) is not only that this disease has dominated the decade, truncated gay lives and gay life, produced both physical and psychological casualties, taken some and (apparently) not others, produced arguments over what the real cause is, but—staggering as it may seem after the expenditure of so much blood, energy, and effort—nobody really knows even now why some people have "survived" and some have not. The friend in New York who is, of all the people I know, most privy to the latest theories, gossip, treatments, has always impressed me, when I asked at various times the past several years, "Is this the cure?" "Is that the cause?" "Was that how he got it?" and "What would *you* personally take?" by answering, with a sigh, "I don't know."

Ignorance—the inability to solve a problem, the weariness that comes with failed attempts to—is not something people are generally comfortable with. Like children who cannot get a turtle to come out of its shell, they eventually leave the insoluble enigma and go on to something they can decipher, and replace that problem with newer, less intractable ones. The current silence is really that of science. Those announcements of new drugs that used to appear in the news, one after the other, and cause such a stir, do not come so frequently anymore. Doctors speak of AIDS as a "manageable disease," like diabetes; something, that is, one can live with, as if everyone has given up the idea of a magic bullet, a final end to this—as if AIDS is going to be relegated to the shelf on which those other, long-term, debilitating afflictions lie: multiple sclerosis and dystrophy and Lou Gehrig's and cystic fibrosis—the telethon diseases. This weekend, memorial marches will be held for those lost to AIDS—an annual remembrance, like Memorial Day itself. It all settles into a way of life.

And yet those who will live this way, in this brave new world, are not really able to, according to the article in the *Los Angeles Times*. They do not believe they are uninfected, it says; they do not believe safe sex or celibacy will prevent their being infected; they think it would be egocentric to imagine they've been "spared"; they lie to friends who've tested Positive about their test results; they lose friends who don't believe they can understand what they're going through; they think their psychological problems (guilt, depression) are not important compared to others. For such people, says Dr. James Titchener at the University of Cincinnati, "the sub-conscious mind's irrational sense of guilt is telling them that they do not deserve to enjoy life when others around them suffer and die." Many of them, says John Acevedo, a psychologist who works with the AIDS Health Project in San Francisco, "have withdrawn socially or sexually. 'In their attempts to avoid more pain, and in some cases to avoid infection, they isolate. They shut down completely,' he says." Like the man described in the article's opening paragraph: "Three years ago, after he had watched his five best friends die of AIDS, interior designer David Ramey fled his native San Francisco to begin a new life across the bay in Walnut Creek. 'I moved to the suburbs and became a hermit,' he says."

While some of the "survivors" have given up mainstream jobs to work full-time for AIDS fund-raisers, or participate in experimental vaccine programs, the majority of them—which means the majority of gay men in this country, the article points out— have, I suspect, moved physically or emotionally to some version of Walnut Creek. And so you get, near the close of the eighties, a splintering of homosexual America into millions of individual fates, different positions in relation to AIDS, and a sense that everyone has made his little bargain with fate and adjusted to all of this as best he can. And this is the way things are going to be, for a long, long time.

Yet nothing is really resolved—which is one of the hardest characteristics of the plague to accept. Like the war in Vietnam, which military men predicted Americans would never support, because democracies do not tolerate long, drawn-out guerrilla wars, AIDS is something we would just as soon have off our TVs. It is now quite literally a commercial, in fact, a little film that comes on during station breaks, like the clip about drunk driving. But AIDS is not something we can withdraw from, as

America did from Vietnam. It may be over, as news, as a shocking, horrifying novelty; it may be something we can remove from the media, or stop talking about or brooding about because that doesn't seem to help. But it's not going away so long as the virus continues to spread. There may be no way of predicting the future (personal or public), but people will go on, as in wartime, under its influence. They will grow used to the rationing (of sex), and the dangers, and the deaths of friends, and the possibility of disaster. They will take what pleasures they can, where they can, and drift in and out of bouts of anxiety and depression, and then take a renewed interest in life. They will adapt.

In 1984 a friend compared the plague to a shark attack—and that's just what it was like, initially: a beach party, a group of people swimming along (quite literally at places like Fire Island) who suddenly saw one another disappearing. No one knew what was going on, and no one had time to think. Now they can—about the unfairness, the irrationality of fate, about how much is still mysterious, and how much there is still to come, about how they have adjusted—because people do adjust, to anything. AIDS has lost its urgency in the national consciousness. Science seems stuck. And everyone would like to say, "It's over," even though it's not. Eight years into the plague, in fact, almost everything has lost its immediacy—except the news that a friend has just had a seizure in a taxi in London. (Brain tumor. Not long to live. Better say goodbye now.) Then the original horror, the anger, the grief, the outrage return—and this lull, this banality, seems even more bizarre.

The Incredible Shrinking City

S OME THINGS DO not disappear: the people on St. Marks Place who somehow express something in themselves by laying out on a thin blanket forty-five back issues of *Honcho*, and seven hardback books, and stand there all night waiting to sell one of them—they're still here, in greater numbers, it seems, since the outdoor bazaar now spreads westward all the way to Astor Place and south to Seventh Street. Walking back to the apartment now requires a sort of delicate ballet, especially if you want to pass the pedestrians in front of you, in that small, faster-flowing space between the strollers and the vendors straddling their blankets at curbside. If you're really in a hurry—or suddenly claustrophobic in the press of all these gawkers and faux-merchants—then you've got to dash between the two *en pointe*, without stepping on a single magazine. Getting to the apartment building now is like crossing a finishing line: Once the door closes behind, it's victory—peace and quiet. St. Marks Place is empty now only very late at night—divinely empty; the merchants, their blankets, childlike collections of found objects, gone. How they make money I don't know, why they do it, I know less. But they've been here for the past six years, and they're not going away.

Others are. Years ago people talked of having to edit their phone books—rip out whole pages—but at the time I did not relate to this very much. This time I come back to New York with my list of addresses and phone numbers, and I do. The people I cannot call, the friends I cannot go see, for the first time equal in number the ones I can. Some have moved away—to Los Angeles, Long Island, upstate. Others are obsessed with new things (jobs, Act Up). Others are making new friends to replace the ones they've lost. But most are just gone. Eddie, who died first; Rhodes, who surprised us by dying; Robert—whose absence we're still not used to. "It's like with Barry," a friend says over lunch. "I have this urge to say: 'All right, you've done this long enough now. Come back.'" The fact that he's not coming back, as time goes by, expands rather than shrinks. This time, too, there's Emmanuel—or rather, there's not Emmanuel. His widow, and roommate, are living in his loft now. I think of calling her, but don't. What would we talk about? Emmanuel. His memorial service, who came, who spoke. Eventually we would have to hang up. And he would be no more there at the end of the phone call than he was at the beginning.

On Monday I walk over to his building instead. It's mid-afternoon; I stop half a block away at the tiny intersection of two streets at the southwestern edge of Soho, and look up. Knowing what went on in the loft—the death of his lover, and then Emmanuel, after a considerable struggle—I expect the windows to look different from those on the floor above or below: sepulchral cavities exuding a spectral air. But they don't. In fact, there is no trace of what was endured and defied there. *If these walls could talk* is the expression; but these walls do not. The windows on the sixth floor look out on a mild fall afternoon broken by the cries of some boys playing basketball at the end of Thompson Street. Otherwise there is nothing. Emmanuel doesn't live there anymore. You can't play with him. Nor does Matthew. Or Matthew's mother who came east to nurse her son. All three actors in an unbelievable tragedy, gone.

Standing there in the unseasonable warmth, however, I imagine pressing the buzzer, hearing Emmanuel's voice on the intercom, seeing the smile that greets me after walking up five flights to his loft, the same smile that is now on the dust jacket of his book, *Mortal Embrace*. I hear too *"Bon jour"*, as I leave my shoes just inside the door, follow him back into the kitchen for the chicken or steak he always prepared, and then the conversation after dessert as he hooks himself up to his portable IV—conversation mostly, the last year, about his book: its discovery by an editor at Farrar, Straus, the praise from Susan Sontag and Richard Howard, the publication in France, the trip back to Paris to appear on the TV show *Apostrophes*—the literary excitement that made Emmanuel's struggle with AIDS almost glamorous. I miss the visits, this excitement, these long talks, but mostly I miss Emmanuel, and it is strange to turn away finally and realize he's not in that building on Thompson Street anymore, that I cannot ring the buzzer and go up.

Nor can I visit Robert—and, since he lived on the Upper West Side, it seems too macabre to take the IRT uptown to walk past his building, on its tree-lined block of brownstones. That *would* be silly. Yet it seems incredible that the sunless, lamplighted living room is no longer one whose door will open for me. (After calling first, of course. Who answers 663-1244 now?) After Robert's death, a friend said he could not imagine other people in the apartment; said it should be installed intact in a museum. It is: the museum of my mind. And since I can summon up quite clearly the sight of Robert, or Michael, offering me a basket of muffins while their phone rings, there would be no point in walking past their doorway. The same doorman would, I'm sure, be slouched in the dim gray lobby watching a baseball game on his portable TV, but their names, in fancy script, would not be above the buzzer, and I could not walk up the stone stairs to the second floor, knock, and have the door swing back to reveal one, or both of them, standing there with bright eyes and slightly comic expressions, like adults on Christmas Day, you, their guest, the present they are about to unwrap in conversation. Someone else lives there now; who I don't know, or care to. In New York one could write novels simply listing over the years the tenants of an apartment.

All of this I resent. I know that each time I come back, New York has changed, and I have, too, but the evisceration of what was constant (Emmanuel, Robert) has gone too far this time— not only Emmanuel and Robert, but the people I knew through them. Each time a friend dies or moves away, so do six acquaintances. There is a story by John O'Hara called "Teddy and His

Friends" about a (presumably gay) man liked by a number of people who have nothing in common, they realize after he dies, but their friendship with him. Emmanuel brought me Jean Michel, Jorge, Kristine, Patricio, Tony, the last two part of a crazy group of Argentines who went back and forth between Paris and New York. Robert brought me Stephen, George, Robert W., Barry. Some were friends I introduced to Robert; but having lost Robert, our own friendship is altered—because it had grown to include him. His disappearance now weakens all those ties. One day reading the *Times* I come upon an article about the apartment on Fifth Avenue in which Robert's memorial service was held. The article is about the aviary in the apartment and the trompe l'oeil ceiling in the dining room. (Death takes an instant; style is forever.) My first reaction is: I must send this to George, who misses Robert even more than I. But I don't. It too seems pointless, like calling Emmanuel's widow; the reason for the connection is gone.

And so—with editions of the newspaper that continue to appear daily after we die—the city goes on without its missing persons. There are replacements. My new roommate has a lover at last; they get up each day and cook elaborate breakfasts punctuated with hugs and kisses; but each morning I leave the apartment for another round of visits to museums, lunches with friends, walks, outings. I keep running into these holes in the landscape, and finally I realize melancholy is going to be the mood of this visit, whether I approve of it or not. Of course it's wrong. Of course it's nostalgic. Of course it's indulgent. But I can't seem to snap out of it. Because each time I come back, it's friends I want to see first. This October it was Emmanuel, and Robert, for some reason; and they're gone. And now, as I walk the city, the others who're not there to call or have lunch with begin to step forward.

They've named a corner off Sheridan Square in honor of Charles Ludlam. I'm glad. But there are many corners, doorways, buildings in New York now that memorialize people without an official designation. Walking through Madison Square I think of Cosmo—whose windows overlook the park. The canopy of 96 Fifth Avenue means Eddie. The bus going down Fourteenth Street, Rhodes—he used to take it from the gym to his apartment on Avenue C, get off it if he saw me on the sidewalk, and say, "Greetings! What's the dish?" On our way to the Gaiety one night, sitting in a deli on Thirty-fourth Street, one of us says—raising a pickle to his lips—"Friday is the anniversary of Rhodes's death. He'll be dead two years." Suddenly I feel like I'm part of that coterie of old Jewish men at the Y who sit on the bench at the racquetball court joking about friends who are no longer there. The man who mentioned Rhodes takes a bite of his pickle, and goes on to describe Junior, his new boyfriend, but our little gathering does not feel quite the same after that. Why? We're missing Rhodes, in both senses.

Later that week at the Metropolitan Museum at the Velázquez show, oppressed by mobs in front of his paintings, I retreat to the cool, empty rooms devoted to Islamic art—a perfect refuge, shadowy and still, where I look at the woven things on the walls and think: Ocsi used to buy textiles like these and sell them to collectors. In the doorway of the room from a seventeenth-century house in Damascus, listening to the water splash in the little fountain, I think of him again. The beauty and serenity remind me of his calm good humor. The view from a bench in the Rambles afterward, where we used to run into each other, makes the title of a Samuel Beckett play run through my head: *Happy Days*. So that I'm reassured that I'm not crazy when a friend, after dinner a few evenings later, says as he shakes his head and taps his cigarette against the ashtray, "We had the best times. The best times."

Everyone feels that way about his youth, no doubt—but this time it's not just nostalgia. People and places *have* disappeared. The city *is* shrinking. New York *is* strangely haunted. The neighborhood I live in, its sidewalk covered with magazines and old LPs, is more crowded than ever, congested in a way it was not ten years ago. The Act Up meeting I go to Monday night is jammed with an exhilarating mix of men and women, all ages, types, milieus; the energy is intoxicating. People are beginning to have sex again, I'm told, because they assume that if AIDS has not got them by now, it's not going to. The parties at the Saint have resumed. Rumors have Michael Fesco opening a new club. The park on Fifteenth Street is cruisy again; a man tries to pick me up. But over his shoulder I'm staring at the facade of a hospital at the park's north end, where a friend was trapped for weeks before he died. At a certain point, one simply knows too much.

That's it. Everyone engineers the particular mix of past, present, and future he wants in life—by staying, or moving away; changing, or keeping, a job; acquiring, or losing, friends—but this time the city has silted up with the Past. New York has always seemed to me a marvelous stage set in which different companies of actors get to do their roles, and then depart; but there is a dreadful moment, I'm beginning to realize, when the floor show you came to see is over. Nothing brings this home more to me than the news that the Ridiculous Theatrical Company is now doing Charles Ludlam's first play—without Ludlam. Brave move. What else can the remaining members of the company do? Yet I cannot imagine these plays without him, and I think, each time I walk past the corner named for him, that honors do not really compensate for the loss of genius, or any person who brought you joy, for that matter. This time Manhattan reminds me of something I've always known but didn't want to believe: That one part of us exists only in the form of people we love and who love us. The rest of the world is backdrop. The rest of the world really is just a stage.

But the show, of course, must (literally) go on—which is why the Ridiculous Theatrical Company is doing *The Big Hotel*—and why I end up staying in the apartment a bit longer each morning while my roommate and his lover make breakfast. It's not just that we're getting used to each other. It's the sight of two people lodged in that most salubrious medium (the Present), making their version of the memories I've been wallowing in and can't seem to shake loose this visit. They met at a party, took a share this summer in a house on Fire Island where everyone had a nickname, live and go to the gym together, plan to visit Los Angeles for Christmas, make French toast every morning—like the people who now live in Emmanuel's and Robert's apartments, perhaps—and sit at the kitchen table eating together, while I skim a book review in the *Times* of Umberto Eco that makes me want to call Robert to ask if there is something in the Italian imagination that runs to plots, secret societies, conspiracy theories. Eventually they get up to do the dishes. And hug each other. All I can think—the Brooding Queen watching them from the other room—is: They're kissing now right where A. lay on the floor decomposing after he took his overdose. ("Did the man who lived here before have AIDS?" my roommate asks one day. "No," I say, "but he thought he did.") How time flies! How Life, its generations, goes on; superimposed on top of the previous, like the cities from different epochs the archaeologists found while looking for Troy in Anatolia. Do my roommate and his lover need to know of the people who lived here before they did? Did I know anything about the people who preceded me? Of course not. Why should we? Yet this time, I know. And the knowledge is so heavy this time in New York, my roommate asks why I seem "less enthusiastic" this visit. I say it's my writing. But it's really, I think, the fact that, this time, the number of people I can't call equals the number of people I can. So while I sit there leafing through the newspaper—going over in my head the fact that I can't see Emmanuel or Robert—I wonder if either of them knew how much I'd miss him after he died. How could he? I didn't know myself.

My roommates dress, say good-bye, and set out into the city— a single unit, two entering the world as one—and moments later the phone rings. "John just left," I say, "shall I tell him who called?"

"Would you?" the caller says. "Tell him—*Dewdrop* called."

"Dewdrop?" I say, writing this down on a pad.

"Yes," he says, with just the hint of a laugh in his voice.

Thank God for the young, I think after hanging up. Someone has to have drag names.

Walking New York

Y EARS AGO, SOMEONE leaving Manhattan for a job in Hong
Kong said, when I asked how he could bear to leave the city,
that it made no difference; when he came back, five or ten years
later, everyone would be doing exactly the same thing—standing
in the Eagle holding a beer, leaning against the wall. He was
right. The Spike seems to have surpassed the Eagle in terms of
popularity, but the Eagle is still the Eagle, and you go back and
forth between the two of them on a cold winter night, glancing
across the street trying to remember just where the nooks and
crannies were underneath the West Side Highway where knots of
men gathered to have sex in the early seventies. The Eagle and the
Spike one can always count on: The men look the same, the milieu
is exactly what it always was. The thrill, and monotony, of standing
in these bars are unchanged, too; and, when you leave, the walk
home—across the blank, dimly lighted expanse of Twenty-second
Street, past the first beautiful facades of townhouses (whose

lanterns may burn a little brighter now, for purposes of crime detection), past the Empire Diner, down to whichever avenue you choose to whatever cross street appeals to you next, past a new place, the Sound Factory Bar, probably worth going into (but you don't), then down Eighth Avenue for a few blocks, since that has become a clone corridor crowded with handsome men, then Eighteenth Street all the way to Broadway. There are new bars near Broadway, too, bars with big glass windows and heterosexual customers, but the rug store is still opposite Paragon, also unchanged, and the wonderful beauty of walking downtown on a cold Sunday night in winter is exactly as it always was. The quiet, the emptiness, the solitude are extraordinary: This huge beast of a city is as gentle as a lamb. Everyone's crashing, getting ready for work the next day, as the same particles in the sidewalk sparkle under the streetlights: Gramercy Park, Irving Place, a couple on the corner discussing how they should go home together, then Third Avenue, then the park at Stuyvesant Place, dark and lovely under its bare trees and a light dusting of snow, with two men cruising. Then down to Second Avenue, over to First, where there are more new groceries and bodegas open late, and more fruit stands, of course, and more restaurants and more gay men. Past the Tunnel, down First Avenue, past the old Club Baths (now a bar called Stella's, outside of which you stop to watch some cute Hispanic men playing pool where the lockers of the baths used to be), past the little grocery on the corner of Houston, where a patient man of Andean aspect stands outside, guarding the produce and opening the door for you when you finally pick up a paper and two grapefruits and head inside to pay for them, and then a new popular restaurant on the corner itself, where, under the streetlight, you finally make eye contact with a beautiful young man with short, black hair, dark eyes, carrying a gym bag, who may be straight or gay, you can't tell.

Walking in New York is a form of theater—*the* form of theater the city offers, and always has—and walking New York as a gay man means, inevitably, cruising. Cruising, when you are young, makes every walk—to the grocery, or post office—fraught with possibility. On Bank Street one slushy afternoon, I see a young man coming toward me with beautiful wavy hair, clear eyes, pale skin, as fresh on that grimy street as a field of snow in Vermont; and I realize, or recall, just what it means to walk about the city when one looks like that. When you are older, however, you begin to notice yourself, as you walk the city, vanishing, bit by bit, like the Invisible Man, in the faces that don't look at you. Still, there are always lots of faces to look at. There are Asian faces on Orchard Street, where I'm staying this time, and, around the corner, Puerto Rican faces, and, down Allen Street, at East Broadway, Chinese faces, and then, past City Hall, into the maw of Wall Street, every kind of face. There is around some of these faces a gay uniform: black leather jacket, faded jeans, baseball cap worn backward (the latter even at the baths). Fashions, like generations, seem to last a decade, so the baseball cap is with us for a few more years. So is short hair (which, on the young, looks young, and on the old, gay). There's the East Village clone, and the Chelsea clone, and the very buffed, model/actor/waiter look one sees in the restaurant at Eighth and Eighteenth, where, my friend Victor tells me on our way to the McBurney Y, all the boys go. They do. We press our faces against the glass and peer at them, the way one looks at fish in an aquarium, and then go on. The McBurney Y is also the same—the lobby slightly rearranged, but otherwise, the feeling on a Saturday afternoon is exactly what it always was: the slightly seedy, sexy silence, the gleam of smooth stone, faint echoes, people descending the stairs fresh from a workout, pausing in the lobby to wrap scarves around their necks before taking their stimulated bodies out into the cold.

The cold is dry, exhilarating, the reason, I suspect, New York is New York—the thing residents get sick of by the middle of February, but which, to a visitor, is deeply energizing. Of course there are other reasons for the feeling of excitement—mainly the street life. Cities other than New York are oozing out on all sides now with new subdivisions, new expressways, more strip malls, glassy office buildings that regard splashing fountains in office parks set beside expressways in the middle of nowhere: Edge City—all variations on the automobile, all deserts without a scintilla of street life. The polar opposite of Manhattan, where there is only one place to expand—up—and where old neighborhoods, because of that, get revitalized by new populations, and a single storefront becomes, over the ten years you return on visits, a bar, a gallery, a clothes store, the sidewalks around it providing more eye contact, more stimulation, more information per square block than any other city I know. The information may be crushingly monotonous when you live there. It may even be startlingly the same, when you come back. But it's much more stimulating than the vacuum, the social void, in which people live—or rather, drive cars—in Edge City.

One night I walk up from Houston to Ninetieth Street and Central Park West—around seven o'clock, when Fifth Avenue is still thronged with people; another evening, I walk down Third Avenue to Orchard Street from Fifty-seventh Street; back and forth to Soho and the West Village almost every other day; but mostly, this time, I find myself turning south when I leave the building, and heading down to Wall Street.

This walk is new to me—through a part of town that used to intimidate me slightly, when I lived on St. Marks Place—but this time, as with so much that frightens us in life, I see there is nothing to be afraid of at all. The atmosphere is the one the East Village used to have. The East Village is now middle class and filled with young people; Avenue A now looks better than First or Second. There are new bars, restaurants, up and down it. But south of Houston, down Chrystie and Allen and Orchard, the landscape has that abandoned, bombed-out look it used to have north of Houston. Orchard Street is absolutely dark at night: the stores closed, a single light burning above the doorway of the building I return to, the only person on the block. Walking down Allen Street, past the bare trees that line the park that bisects the avenue, one has the feeling one used to have on St. Marks in the early seventies. Walking south the faces change from Puerto Rican to Chinese—the language, too—and soon you find yourself in Chinatown; Greater Chinatown, expanding and spilling over its old confinement to Mott Street—where faces, fish, vegetables, stores, letters suddenly become more vivid, strange, and self-contained. Then, heading toward the World Trade Towers, you wend your way through narrow, angled streets toward City Hall, and, if you have a mind, up onto the Brooklyn Bridge—at dusk, or afterward—for a view that ranks, especially when night is falling, with the Pyramids, the Grand Canyon, or whatever is on your list of show-stopping sights; and then, back on to Manhattan, and the Wall Street Sauna.

Then back to Orchard Street, up Rivington, Madison, Grand, Ludlow, Forsythe, Eldridge, Delancey, getting lost, passing projects, and streets of tenements occupied by teenage girls sitting on stoops talking in accents that do not change, and constitute New York, back to your corner, on which a bright-eyed Puerto Rican youth tearing at a Danish walks back and forth, looking at you with shining eyes, eyes you would love to make contact with, till you see another man come up and make an exchange with him that means he is on the corner dealing crack; while just across Houston, at First Avenue and First, the *jeunesse dorée* are looking at each other romantically over candles on the tables of the restaurant on the corner. You look at the Puerto Rican; he looks at you. But instead of meeting him, you buy the *Times*, and go upstairs to bed.

When you get up the next day, you raise the blinds, and lie in bed watching a cold blue sky; a pillow case flapping on a windowsill; a man in an apartment building across Houston who keeps opening his window, sticking his head out, then closing it; two cats sunning themselves on the snow in the rubble-filled backyard; and, finally, seagulls that swoop across the space between your window and Houston Street. Lying in bed in New York in perfect solitude is a luxury because you know that when you wish to leave that bed, there is all that life waiting for you outside.

Yet most of it is somewhat déjà vu; which is why one just keeps walking. When you stop walking, you call a friend to see if you can visit—which may be the real unstated pleasure that anchors these walks, gives them a focal point. Everyone you drop in on, it seems, can be divided into two groups—those who have withdrawn, because of the ravages of AIDS, or middle age, or the synergistic combination of the two; and those still participating, still playing the game, still out there running around. Which category you belong to has to do with factors both external and internal: age and its transformations, and temperament. Two bowls in which people's names can be placed: Stopped Living, and Still Running Around. The former has to do with Survivor's Syndrome—as a character in Paul Rudnick's new play *Jeffrey* makes clear, in a stinging speech to the lead. Is it possible to stop living when you are still alive? Do you stop living when you stop having sex? "You give out the message that you are not to be considered," says a friend, about walking the streets of New York. "You make it impossible to be approached." He's right. It's self-protective, of course, but also a reaction primarily to the fact that one doesn't feel worth approaching. People are still approached, however. One day I walk the Village with a handsome thirty-year-old and watch the response: the sidelong, furtive glance at the last minute; the frank, warm smile; the turning back to look (sometimes immediately, sometimes after they've crossed the street, to retain their dignity). Heads still turn. People are still having sex.

One friend I visit has two boyfriends—one scheduled to come by at five, the other at seven, the evening I drop in—and cannot decide which to continue with and which to end. On Saturday afternoon, he tells me, when I come in out of the cold, that he's thinking of dumping B., who takes too many drugs, has too pronounced a Long Island accent (for some, an aphrodisiac!), and is too eager to get married. The newer one has a gorgeous body, a huge dick, and is very hot sex. The next evening, after dates with both, the descriptions are reversed: The first one is truly devoted, handsome, hot sex, and willing to correct his flaws, even to the point of taking diction lessons. The second is, really, a queen. He plays their voices on the answering machine for me. The next evening, after going to the theater with my friend and Boyfriend No. 2, I leave them in front of his building on lower Fifth Avenue (still the most picture-perfect sidewalk in New York), in the slushy snow, on their way up in the elevator to his place. Ah, New York: between the theater, and lovemaking, a walk.

The next night I drop by another friend's and watch him dress for a concert he always attended with his best friend—who died a year ago—and cannot help but think: He's going alone. Alone. This man who used to know so many people: all dead. *So get new ones,* someone says to him on the street one day when he describes his predicament. He never speaks to that person again. "It was like saying: Go out and get another baby to kill and eat. I was astonished. Friends can't be replaced!" Of course they have to be, if one wishes to have friends. And they will be, I suspect, when he leaves this city that has so many memories for him they crush the life out of it, this city whose streets are all lined with buildings in which someone used to live, used to be handsome—the city he has decided to abandon, to start a new life, elsewhere. "Everything's so *old*," says another friend I meet on Thirteenth Street to walk around the East Village with my last night. (He's waiting for his boyfriend to get out of prison; perhaps that will make things new again.) It's hopeless, and poignant, trying to keep up these friendships that circumstances have left so high and dry, so distant from the context in which they were formed. But they are all one has left; one can only mark changes in people one has known a long time. And, like the city, whose neighborhoods die, lie fallow, then come to life again, like individual storefronts, for that matter, these lives are variegated: Some shut down, are replaced; some remain almost as they were; others renovate to keep up with new styles; some busy, some nearly unvisited. (We go to New York, after all, to merchandise ourselves; the analogy is almost exact.) And when you leave them, you're walking again, past new people, new faces, new restaurants, new bars. When the crush of memory, the sense of déjà vu, the changes in yourself become confusing, you can always set out again—someplace— and walk. Just walk. And walk. Losing one's confusion, suspending one's depression, in the cold air, the somber slums, the figure of a man in a hooded parka coming toward you in the fitful light of store windows, a man who may or may not be the one to make you feel new again, detached from your past, in this city of fixed character and oh so painful change.

Bobby's Grave

THE CEMETERY IS one I've driven by for years, on my way to the beach—it sits atop a hill just behind the funeral home, conspicuous, as all funeral homes in small towns are, for its neatness, and its imposing architecture. It should not have been a surprise when I learned that this funeral home would be handling Bobby's burial, but still it felt odd finally to turn in at an establishment one had driven by for nearly ten years. The day of the funeral was sunny and clear; the sort of day graduations occur on up north—the grass a deep, intense green, roses in bloom, bright sunlight. It was a grim occasion nevertheless—his friends from childhood weeping at the grave while the priest spoke to his mother and lover, seated side by side in the front row of folding chairs under the canopy. (In a small town in north Florida, a black priest presiding over the funeral of a gay man at which the mother and boyfriend are seated side by side indicates that social change really does trickle down. The florist asked his mother as he prepared the flowers, "So young! What did he die of?" "AIDS," she said, and lectured the clerk at the state records office who assumed she wouldn't want AIDS listed as the cause of death.) Like all funerals, it was very social; the last time, I kept thinking, I would see these people together, people I had come to know through Bobby, and could not imagine knowing without him.

Five weeks later I found myself driving to the beach through the town on a hot July afternoon, and I turned in to the cemetery to see if the tombstone had been put up. There was only one other car in the place—a man in a Plymouth Valiant on his way out, who passed me with a sad expression as I held my hand up to acknowledge him. I parked under the shade of some tall pines and walked barefoot down the dirt road that led to the graves. The cemetery is pretty—set on a plateau near Highway 16, enclosed by dense woods, the center treeless and open, the rest punctuated with laurels and tall pines; not the skinny pines planted close together down here so they will grow a size convenient for paper mills, but real pines, allowed to reach a great width and height. The pine tree is magnificent when left like that— unencumbered, casting a deep and fragrant shade beneath its outstretched branches. That was the sort of pine that shaded the graves I walked among.

The first thing that caught my eye as I walked in the general direction of what memory told me was the place Bobby was buried was a green tent, like the one erected for Bobby's funeral. When I could not find Bobby's grave, I walked over to it and learned why the man who'd passed me on his way out had worn so pained a face. Someone had just died. A funeral had just been held, that morning; the second half of a married couple whose tombstone was already in place, the husband dead since 1978, the wife laid in the ground that morning, her date of death not yet chiseled into the granite. She had survived her husband by fifteen years. The tent still shaded the mound of earth left above her interred coffin; the bunches of flowers numbered more than thirty, arranged in a sort of U-shape along both sides of the canopy, the tombstone itself a large one. The overwhelming impression was one of abandonment. They've gone off and left her, I thought—unable to see or smell the flowers heaped in her honor. This woman, I thought, will never again be told to finish her peas, or go to school, or come downstairs and meet so-and-so. No one will ever call, or make any demand on her again. Some of the flowers looked so fresh it was a mystery how they'd managed to retain their color and form in the July heat. Some were flowers I could not identify, so I bent down and removed the card stuck on a plastic prong florists insert in bouquets. On one side was the sender's name, on the other a preprinted list used to identify the order, with blank spaces for the type of flower, sender, destination, type. These flowers were silk—which explained their durability. The breeze blew over them all, through the deep shade under the canopy, onto the blazing green meadow. All these people had been here this morning, like us, that morning five weeks ago; all of them were probably back at someone's house now, eating ham, drinking iced tea, talking with the sad eyes and nervous volubility of a funeral party—that odd mixture of heavy feet and lighthearted chatter, that rich, rich, mixture of emotions. One of them—the man in the Valiant—had already come back to the grave site.

Perhaps her son, his eyes strained, near tears, at leaving her there. Sons are expected to care for mothers; one of the things that bothered Bobby, I suspect, was the fact that he would not be able to take care of his, those last few weeks when he was so sick and so furious at what was happening to him that he turned his face to the wall and refused to speak to anyone.

I walked over to the section where I felt certain Bobby had been buried, but could not find his name on any of the stones. There were many markers, all the same pale gray granite. Surely it was this stand of pines I stood beneath. No, that one. And so on. (Tombstones settle, a friend told me; they sink, and have to be raised up; his own father's sank, and when they raised his father's, his mother's and aunt's sank lower. He would have to take care of it. "Will you be buried next to them?" I asked. "Yes," he said, "I got mine when I got my mother's. I just wanted to take care of it, and show her, I think, I wasn't afraid of death.") (I am.)

Nobody believes in his own death, said Freud. Too true. When I finally found, to my relief, a stone that had Bobby's surname on it—his father's—I saw what I'd been looking for: the coffin-shaped mound of cracked, dried, light brown dirt under which Bobby lay, a sprig of artificial red flowers stuck into it with a black wire. Here he was. Lying, under the dirt, not sitting up in a rocking chair on the porch talking to me, as he did when I stopped by on my way to the beach the past several years. In retrospect, Bobby seems that rarest, most wonderful thing: fun. More rare than we suppose, I thought, as I stood there thinking of all the people I knew down here. Witty, honest, down-to-earth, sometimes malicious, perceptive, great fun to sit and talk with, about others or himself. Only now he was not in a chair on the porch. He was under the ground. Along with, I thought, all that virus. Finally defeated. No longer replicating. Unable to infect another host. Finished. Stopped. Dead. End of the line. Along with the CMV and toxo and MAI. At what point did the cellular activity of all these organisms cease? The minute the heart stopped beating, or later, in the ground?

It doesn't matter; it's such a stupid question; I think it only because it's what put Bobby here, at the ripe age of forty, instead of the rocking chair on the porch. He lies, beneath this mound of tan dirt, next to his father, who also died young, and the space reserved for his mother, now in the Keys. There they are: parents and son, right beside each other—a family unit still, mother, father, child. The acorn did not fall far from the tree. It's touching, the sight of this cluster of graves. It makes me think how nomadic most of us are. Bobby is buried in the town in which he was born and grew up, beside his parents. My friend Cal knows where he'll be buried too—next to his parents, in a town southwest of this one. I don't. I am a product of the corporate culture that has banished death entirely except as a joke on *The Golden Girls*. My parents worked and lived far from their birthplaces, and they never went back. The cemetery of the town they ended up in is the ugliest I've ever seen: a sandy slope surrounded by a chicken-wire fence beside a two-lane highway under the blazing sun. I can't imagine being interred there. This one is actually beautiful—on what might be called, in Florida, a hill, like something in *Our Town*. It's the closed circle of a family's little romance. It's where Bobby lies beside his father, because his mother—the day she had to buy a spot for her husband—seeing that Bobby was not likely to marry, bought one for him, too.

It's a cliché by now to say that our culture has banished death from its consciousness, its daily life, its rituals. It's equally banal to say that AIDS has forced many Americans to experience death at an age and in a way they never expected to. The Egyptians built pyramids and furnished their tombs with artifacts for the afterlife. We get cremated, have a cocktail party, and go out to Fire Island. We're too sensible to dwell on Death. Some of the old-fashioned ceremonies were, in fact, gruesome. Some of the new ones are hilarious. In Gaultier, Mississippi, the paper says today, a funeral home has built a drive-in window—much like a bank—so that mourners can lean out their car window, push a button, and see the dead person lying in the back of a building on a color video monitor. A rival funeral director warned that joy-riding teens might want to be "entertained by the appearance of a dead body." On drugs, no doubt. Basically, we don't believe in the afterlife. So what's the point? Death is just a moment that ends all the moments that have preceded it. Or so it seems. In reality, it haunts us just as much as the Egyptians. These accumulated disappearances of people we love. We wonder still: Where did they go—anyplace? Or are they just decomposing molecules without a consciousness? The Catholics are allegedly "good at Death." They were the day Bobby was put into the ground. There is no substitute for those words, that rite. All our lives, no matter how shallow, advertising-soaked, consumerist, come back to it. There's an advertisement on TV down here for a funeral home in Gainesville: A handsome, middle-aged man with a local twang comes on TV once a week and announces community events—fund-raisers, baseball games, club meetings—with an old-fashioned friendliness that draws on our nostalgia for the nineteenth century (which was obsessed with Death—cf. Emily Dickinson, Walt Whitman). Then he makes his pitch for a prepaid funeral contract—like the one my father had, which came in very handy when he died. Yet when I imagine phoning Mr. Williams and signing on the dotted line myself, I'm stuck with the consequences of my life. Whom do I know down here? Who would come—relatives from out of state? Where would I be buried? Next to whom? All these thoughts—like deciding whom you leave your money to— force us to face the fact that lives come to an end, form a little shape, have substance, and are actually weighed, by ourselves, or others, if not our Maker, as we once believed.

I'm sure Bobby thought about all this; what he thought I do not know. At any rate, he's gone, and only we have to deal with his—and so many others'—absence. Bobby's death put a punctuation mark, a period, on the lives of everyone who knew him; this cannot be denied. It put everything in a new perspective. Gone is the worry about car titles, insurance, nurses who would not come back because either the gay "lifestyle," or AIDS, made them uncomfortable, the vomiting, incontinence, changing of sheets, exhaustion, anger, resentment of friends who were not coming by ("People stay away from Death," said the hospice worker), the long, draining, painful vigil. All gone. In their place is sleep under the pines, the silk flowers that never wilt. Bobby's death created a new geography—a new map. All roads are connected now to this spot: his grave. One will never drive past this hill without thinking of him, or stopping to visit. It forms a point on the compass—a fixed foot, around which other journeys, other highways, radiate. Bobby's death left those who remain bitter, sad, judgmental, depressed, withdrawn, forlorn, quiet. Not all deaths are enlightening, though they do throw us back on ourselves. (Read Gerard Manley Hopkins's "Spring and Fall: To a Young Child.") They throw us back on ourselves because, after the death of someone we knew, or loved, we are both more alone and more aware that someday we will die. This knowledge should change things—but it seldom does. Most of us go on doing the same things, only with more anxiety (as Bruce Mailman predicted when asked what effect AIDS would have on sex). Yet there is a deep sea change, beneath the surface. "I'm damaged goods," a friend from New York said after calling to read the obituary of yet another friend there. "There's something inside me that's broken and can never be fixed." A week later, Bobby's partner says almost the same thing: "I'm like a toy I had as a kid that I broke. It could never be fixed. *I* can never be fixed." Later that evening, I find this in what Whitman wrote, after Lincoln died, in "When Lilacs Last in the Dooryard Bloom'd":

> *I saw battle-corpses, myriads of them,*
> *And the white skeletons of young men,*
> *I saw them,*
> *I saw the debris and debris of all the*
> *slain soldiers of the war,*
> *But I saw they were not as was thought,*
> *They themselves were fully at rest,*
> *They suffer'd not.*
> *The living remain'd and suffer'd,*

The mother suffer'd,
And the wife and the child and the musing comrade suffer'd,
And the armies that remain'd suffer'd.

But for the moment, life goes on, which means I leave the cemetery and drive by Bobby's little white house, empty now in the blazing sunlight, so empty, and head for the beach.

Stars

WALKING IS CONSIDERED odd in this little town in the country—but since the laying of a sidewalk last summer, you can go all the way uptown now to the intersection where two highways crisscross each other beneath a traffic light, before the facade of a gas station, a fried-chicken franchise, and a stretch of railroad tracks. The intersection could be anywhere in the United States, anywhere at all, but on the way, you walk past particular things: the insurance agency, the nursery that failed last year in the freeze, the bank, the town hall, and the public park. In the park is a fountain that plashes in the still night for apparently nobody's benefit but my own; at night I am usually the only person out. Sometimes the lights are on above the tennis courts, and people are playing a game or are on the basketball court adjacent to the courts, shooting baskets. Sometimes I make out a solitary teenage boy dribbling a basketball in the dark (the lights now cost twenty-five cents every half hour; in the old days people walked away and left them burning) with the radio on in his car to keep him company. There is also a man who walks his poodle on a leash in his pajamas, and sometimes a policeman is sitting in his car by the public beach waiting for a crime to be committed. Twice I have been accused of a crime—most recently, a woman saw someone walk across her lawn, phoned the cops, and they stopped me and asked to see my footprints. (To take a walk in the United States is to be suspected of either poverty or criminal intent.) Sometimes it is overcast, and in the summer often too humid, but in winter it is mostly clear and dry, and when you finally go up the hill past the public beach and begin the last stretch along the dark, silent gardens of the houses on the lake, you are all alone beneath a cloudless sky. The stars in Florida in the winter are mesmerizing—though it may be merely my imagination, they seem more thickly strewn across the sky than in the summer. Or perhaps the cool air merely leaves one free to look up at them undisturbed—no bugs to swat, no heat to make you want to get indoors to a ceiling fan or air conditioner. In winter, conditions for star watching are perfect; the stars are plenteous and bright, and, if there isn't any moon, you stand there looking up with the distinct feeling that you are on the surface of a planet suspended in space shared by countless others that merely face you, like houses across the lake.

In a small town at night a walk clears the head, gets you out of the house, lets your mind wander, sets you free. I am upset when I meet someone else walking; I have grown accustomed to having the sidewalk to myself as I let unravel in the darkness whatever is on my mind, so that, returning an hour later, whatever facts, events, incidents have made that day good or bad seem to have played themselves out and become a little more ordered than they were on my first receiving them. Sometimes I leave the house after a telephone call from New York. I digest the news—so dense with incident—in the silence exuded by the sleeping gardens. Sometimes the news is bad: A friend is sick, or dead. Tonight I'm told a man committed suicide rather than suffer any longer the deterioration caused by the virus. On the tennis courts I see two couples playing, and some kids on the basketball court beyond, borrowing their light, and the first thing I think about them is, *They do not have It. It has nothing to do with them.* The stars are very white above me when I put the tennis courts behind and go down the hill by the public beach, very thick and beautiful in the black sky—and I think, *R. belongs to that now, a part again of the universe, no longer in human form, a mix of elements, vaporized, cremated, gone, eternal, and dissembled: as unearthly as a star.* And he joins a constellation not marked in the maps of the heavens—of these friends and acquaintances who have now entered the past; I imagine them all out there, white pinpoints of light, stars.

Some of them were stars—to me, or the homosexual world of New York City, or the world in general. Some of them were men who were famous for designing clothes or buildings, or interpreting history, or composing music. Some of them were merely admired on Fire Island. Some were stars in pornographic films—like the man I saw in the slides flashed on the screen of a bar in Washington several years ago, one of the sexual icons of New York, who was in fact withering away even as the men around me paused in the conversation, their drinking, to admire his penis and his pectorals. And now this most recent, newest star: a man so good-looking everyone urged him to become a model, but who chose to remain in publishing, a copywriter, a man from California whose skin, hair, teeth, smile, and bright good looks were startling on the gray streets of Manhattan, whose grime and falling dust could not dim his blondness. He was so blond that unlike everyone else I knew of that hue—whose appearance was affected by age, stress, fast living, the general ash of the urban air—he looked as crisp and golden the last time I saw him as he did the day ten years before when we first met. His western health was a kind of marvel. Why didn't the city get to him? He lived in a house with friends, and former lovers, in the city and commuted to Fire Island in the summers; he was a staple, an icon, of homosexual New York City—handsome but not vain, smart but not mean, blond but not wasted; so that when he got sick, we were all shocked as if it had never happened before, and when he killed himself, we felt a light had been extinguished— and a new star put up in the sky, beneath which I walk on these quiet nights with fear, dread, remorse, sadness, and disgust in the heart. Fear, of It. Dread: Who's next? Remorse: that we should have lived differently. Sadness: that friends suffered. Disgust: that something common as the flu, wretched as African pestilence, could destroy so much that was secure, beautiful, happy; that there should be such penalties for sex. I look at the public beach as I walk by—in a ravine, where a stream issues from another lake. I see a dark grove of live oaks draped with Spanish moss swaying in the breeze, a pale white dock and changing room whose white clapboard sides gleam in the streetlight refracted through the limbs of the trees—and want only one thing: to be alive, and able to swim when the weather gets warm this coming summer.

This ambition is somewhat scaled down from previous ones: I used to take this walk wondering if I should get in the car and drive to Jacksonville and visit the baths and bars. I felt on the loveliest nights—when the moon was new, and there was a soft, warm breeze, and the sensations that characterize a southern night were all in bloom—that such beauty, such a night, required a lover. Then I felt sorry for myself, annoyed that homosexual life was confined to cities, and in those cities to one-night stands. Now I have no such ambitions, do not demand a lover, merely want life. A decrease in expectations, the economists would call it; a rise in conservatism, the politicians; a return to morality, the priests. In fact it is fear and loathing; in reality it is the mind scrambling to accommodate itself to facts beyond its control. The town seems to me as exotic as a colony on the moon because it does not have it. The little old lady who sits alone in her tiny living room in the miniature house so near the sidewalk I can almost reach in through the window and touch her; the solitary adolescent dribbling his basketball on the cement court in the darkness, his bare chest flashing as he passes near the faint radiance of the streetlight; the children who have left their tricycles tilted in the sand of their driveway might as well be living on another planet—and as I walk past the bank whose sign flashes the time and temperature with a loud *clunk*, I feel I can deal with only two facts: *It is nine forty-three, it is sixty-three degrees.* That is all I want to know right now. I don't want any more phone calls, any more news—I have come to detest the sound of a ringing phone.

This shrinking—of the universe to a bank sign on this quiet night—while above me the eerie stars provoke dreary thoughts, this reduction of my dreams to the simple goal of being able to swim this summer, intensifies as the roll call of expiring men expands. As every other day the television or newspaper carries some new fact—300,000 are exposed, Dr. Curran announces; 30,000 will get It in the next five years—one's desires, defiance, beliefs, wilt. One wonders if there isn't some way to fight back—besides celibacy, that is; a treatment of some kind that would allow one to go out and meet the barbarians rather than sit quietly in fear waiting for them to reach the gate. "It's so depressing," a friend says on the phone from New York, after telling me about his arrangements to increase his insurance and make out a will. "You mean all this grown-up stuff," I say. "No," he says, "I mean all this death stuff."

This death stuff is unnerving—one gets up each day, or walks through the quiet town at night, past the two-story houses with lights burning in cozy rooms, and dogs drooping on porches, and bicycles knocked over in the sand, and wonders just how many more facts one will have to absorb. When will it happen? Where do I want to be when it does? How will it happen? Friends say if you don't want to get It, you won't; but this seems to me silly; friends who did not want to die have. Your desire to live one, two, three, or four years is within your power, to a degree; but how much more? And you wonder as you walk through the sleeping town under a sky filled with crystalline stars how this happened, because on quiet nights in winter you have time to think over the past fifteen years and ask, *Could I have lived differently? Been a different kind of homosexual?*

Even as I do, a friend of mine ten years younger is living in the apartment above the first one I lived in, in New York, and writing me letters at three in the morning about the men he has just met, and in some cases slept with—and I thrill to this reenactment of the adventure I had when I moved to the city, and think happily, *It still goes on.* Yet I wonder if this vicarious pleasure is not foolish. In Florida as of February there are thirty-five new cases a month. Thirty thousand are predicted over the next five years in the nation. Promiscuity is, after all, like the engine of some giant ocean liner, which takes days to start once it is stopped. Promiscuity is so huge, so enormous, so habitual, so vital that it is brought to a halt very slowly, and only in the direst of circumstances: the equation of death with sex. There are homosexuals who say promiscuity is our right and cannot be taken away from us, but this sounds like the man on the bridge screaming he has a right to jump. Shut the whole vast machine down, with a shudder, and let us be quiet till this thing is trapped. Because each evening I take this walk, it is pure sentimentality to imagine friends who have disappeared as stars twinkling in the night sky above the Earth—in fact they are just gone.

And the statue to be erected in Sheridan Square of two men on a bench seems oddly outdated now—perhaps a piece of marble with names engraved on it might make more sense. The town beneath these stars does not remember how blond, bright, witty, and well liked R. was; nor does the woman behind the counter of the 7-Eleven store across the railroad tracks whose bright light brings me in out of the darkness. It is open all night. Inside, the woman who works the register on the graveyard shift is talking to a customer buying Tootsie Rolls about a city they have both lived in, San Diego. I buy some cookies, and a wrestling magazine that features foldouts of ten wrestling stars who, both hairy and smooth-chested, wear elaborate belt buckles, tattoos, black bathing suits. It is the sort of magazine a ten-year-old boy or a girl who follows the wrestlers on TV might buy, I guess—neither of which I am, or both of which I am, as I walk home with the magazine folded in my pocket, feeling like a kid who hopes to grow up and have enormous muscles. I guess I still do. Walking home with my cookies, my wrestler magazine, the sound of my footsteps down the quiet street, I have regressed; I might as well be ten; my desires as chaste as stars. And soon I have left the light behind, and pass the boy still dribbling his basketball with an intensity that sounds odd in the deep darkness but comes no doubt from the fact that as he leaps up to make his shot, he too imagines he's a star. Down in the hollow, coming up from the beach, I think the real stars at this moment are the journalists, scientists, volunteers in New York and San Francisco, and wherever else, caring for the men determined to hang on to their human form. And the doctor who delivers us from this thing the brightest star of all. But enough of metaphors. Now the real stars make me stop on the sidewalk and look up: so cold and brilliant, so far away, so unlike anything we know. All that remains beneath them on this planet of hope and dread is the determination to remain terrestrial. All that beats in the stillness of the winter night is the basketball, and the horrified heart.